Taking Care of Yourself

HBR WORKING PARENTS SERIES

*Tips, stories, and strategies for
the job that never ends.*

The **HBR Working Parents Series** supports readers as they anticipate challenges, learn how to advocate for themselves more effectively, juggle their impossible schedules, and find fulfillment at home and at work.

From classic issues such as work-life balance and making time for yourself to thorny challenges such as managing an urgent family crisis and the impact of parenting on your career, this series features the practical tips, strategies, and research you need to be—and feel—more effective at home and at work. Whether you're up with a newborn or touring universities with your teen, we've got what you need to make working parenthood work for you.

Books in the series include:

Advice for Working Dads

Advice for Working Moms

Communicating Better with Everyone

Getting It All Done

Managing Your Career

Taking Care of Yourself

WORKING PARENTS

Tips, stories, and strategies for the job that never ends.

Taking Care of Yourself

Harvard Business
Review Press
Boston, Massachusetts

Cataloging-in-Publication data is forthcoming.

ISBN: 978-1-63369-978-6
eISBN: 978-1-63369-973-1

The paper used in this publication meets the requirements of the American National Standard for Permanence of Paper for Publications and Documents in Libraries and Archives Z39.48-1992.

CONTENTS

Introduction
Self-Care and the Working Parent xiii
Why it's important to take care of yourself.

by Daisy Dowling, Series Editor

Section 1
Give Yourself a Time-Out
Look at How You Spend Your Time

1. Give Yourself Permission to Recharge 3

To care for your children, you need to care
for yourself.

by Elizabeth Grace Saunders

2. Working Dads Need "Me Time," Too 11

They're just as likely to put everyone else first.

by Alyssa F. Westring and Stewart D. Friedman

3. Does Your Schedule Reflect 19
Your Values?

Organize your time around what's
important to you.

by Elizabeth Grace Saunders

Contents

4. Six Ways to Weave Self-Care into Your Workday   27

Tiny changes to your routine can make a big difference.

by Amy Jen Su

5. Do More by Doing Less (at Home and at Work)   35

An exercise to identify unnecessary tasks.

by Kate Northrup

Section 2

Learn to Talk

Communicate Your Needs

6. Four Conversations Every Overwhelmed Working Parent Should Have   45

With yourself, at work, and at home.

by Joseph Grenny and Brittney Maxfield

7. What's a Working Dad to Do?   53

Signal your family commitments to your coworkers.

by Scott Behson

8. **How to Communicate Your**   59
   Self-Care Needs to Your Partner

   Tips for a calm, thoughtful discussion.

   by Jackie Coleman

9. **Too Much to Do? Here's How to**   67
   Ask for Help

   Get the support you need.

   by Heidi Grant

Section 3

Deep Breaths
Check Your Mental and Emotional Health

10. **Stop Feeling Guilty About What**   75
    You Can't Get Done

    Practice self-compassion—and acceptance.

    by Art Markman

11. **How to Refuel When You're Feeling**   81
    Emotionally Drained

    Replenish your energy.

    by Monique Valcour

12. **Let Go of Perfectionism**   91

    It's OK to drop the ball sometimes.

    by Alice Boyes

Contents

13. How Busy Working Parents Can   101
Make Time for Mindfulness

During coffee, meal prep, or your commute.

by Michelle Gale

Section 4

Time for Your Checkup
Prioritize Physical Well-Being

14. How Regular Exercise Helps   109
You Balance Work and Family

It decreases stress and increases self-efficacy.

by Russell Clayton

15. Find Exercise in Life's Margins   115

Every little bit counts.

by Nick Crocker

16. How Working Parents Can   121
Prioritize Sleep

Habits to follow when it feels like you don't
have the time.

by Amie M. Gordon and Christopher M. Barnes

17. Parents, Take Your Sick Days   131

Don't be a martyr.

by Tim Sullivan

Section 5

Recess

Make Your Time Off Matter

18. The Case for Having Hobbies   139

They let you relax, learn, and connect
with others.

by Scott Behson

19. Make Friendships a Part of   147
Your Routine

Spend time together through shared
experiences.

by Neal J. Roese and Kyle S. H. Dobson

20. How to Get the Most Out of   153
a Day Off

Take a break from the day-to-day.

by Elizabeth Grace Saunders

21. Get in the Right State of Mind   159
for Vacation

Unplug, be present, and have fun.

by Alexander Caillet, Jeremy Hirshberg,
and Stefano Petti

Contents

Epilogue

Try It, You Might Like It

22. **It's Not Selfish to Take Care**   169
    of Yourself

    Test it for a month. See how you feel.

    by Stewart D. Friedman

Notes   173
About the Contributors   179
Index   187

INTRODUCTION

Self-Care and the Working Parent

by Daisy Dowling

D o you struggle with how to balance work and family? Are you "always on" in one form or another, whether it's logging in to work, caring for your kids, or handling one of the many other assorted things on your to-do list? How do you take care of *yourself* while doing so?

As an executive coach who specializes in working parenthood, I've counseled hundreds of men and women on effective ways to combine children and career. Just like you, my clients are all hard workers and unassailably devoted to their families. All go to extraordinary lengths to do well at work while really *being there* for their kids, in every sense of the term. Most of them have something else in common, too: a deep sense of uncertainty and unease about also looking after themselves.

If this sounds familiar, it's worth asking yourself whether it's taking a toll on your well-being. To find out, read over the statements below—all ones I commonly hear from men and women in varying careers and family structures, and at all different phases of working parenthood—and see if they strike a chord:

- Of course I'm tired. Between work and the kids, it's impossible to turn off or get any real rest.

- When I do take a break, all I can think about is my to-do list. It's a million miles long, and no matter how many items I cross off of it, it never gets any shorter.

- I used to exercise/meditate/give back to my community/spend time with friends, but I don't have time for that now.

- My productivity isn't anywhere near what it used to be. Maybe that new calendar or organizational system will help . . . or maybe I just need to push myself more.

- Sure, I'd love a break. But I can't skip work and ignore the kids to spend the day at the spa.

- I worry about the wheels coming off the bus. What if I lose it on the job—or at home? I've got to find some way to get a grip.

Comments like these come from a place of diligence and love, of deep and genuine desire to do the right thing. What working parent worth their salt *hasn't* felt as if they should be doing better at work, spending more time with their toddler, or staying more fully available for the kids during the critical teenage years? If you recognize yourself in these voices, it's evidence that your working-parent instincts are good, conscientious ones.

Those instincts, though, can also have a downside. They can lead you to overthink things, to overwork, and eventually neglect the one most important element in making working parenthood work for the long term: you. That, of course, feels lousy, and it also makes working parenthood harder. It's already tough to deliver your best on-the-job performance and show up as the loving parent you want to be each day, but it's even tougher when you're also tired and completely run down. Think about it this way: Would you ever counsel a friend and fellow parent to ignore their own needs for sleep, downtime, and human connection and urge them to "just work harder"? Would you expect that approach to yield great results? If not, why use that approach yourself?

Maybe, like many of the moms and dads I work with, you have bought into the overall *idea* of self-care, but you're not quite sure how to act on it. Getting to that spa or committing to regular yoga sessions (two images that often come to mind when people think of stereotypical self-care) might feel impossible for many different reasons—or might trigger some major working-parent guilt, even if feasible. Ironically, the more committed a parent and professional you are, the more the idea of focusing on yourself feels irresponsible, even wrong.

Let's reframe that by stepping back and clarifying what self-care really means and why it's anything *but* selfish. With my clients, I define working-parent self-care very simply as any habit or practice that feels like you, that you engage with regularly, and that has the effect of increasing your working-parent resilience and satisfaction over the long term. For you personally, self-care might involve exercise, sleep, alone time, social time with friends, watching funny videos on YouTube, or any of a hundred other activities. When your personal battery is drained, that particular self-care practice charges it back up. It has the dual benefit of making you happier *and* allowing you to give more to your work and to your kids. Imagine having a reliable, simple, works-for-you way to be certain you can face the stresses of working parenthood—even just that one important meeting tomorrow, or time with your child this evening—with greater confidence and strength, with more energy and calm. And imagine your clients, colleagues, and your kids getting the benefit of that stronger, more centered you.

This book will help you get there. In the chapters that follow, you'll find dozens of practical, powerful self-care techniques specifically tailored for working parents and recommended by experts and parents alike. These techniques address the concerns and needs most commonly found at the intersection of work and caregiving, including how to focus on your needs and values (and communicate them to others), check in on your emotional and mental well-being, take time for exercise and physical health, and make the most of your time off. The tips and approaches in this book don't require any special resources or force you to make sacrifices in one area of your life to feed the others. In fact, you can fold most of them into your regular routine. And they *work*, immediately. Take Nick Crocker's advice on how to "Find Exercise in Life's Margins" in chapter 15, or use any of Elizabeth Grace Saunders's excellent counsel on managing your time and schedule, and you'll feel more energized and in-control *today*.

The ideas you'll find here are broad. They're applicable whether you have a newborn or school-aged kids, you work full- or part-time, you're a sole caregiver or you have a wide support system. And they're relevant regardless of current context. As I write these words, we're smack in the center of a global pandemic, and like everyone else, I'm cooped up, coping with my second-grader's math curriculum on top of cooking, cleaning, taking care of two kids, and doing my actual job. "Sheltering in place" isn't my average week, but Monique Valcour's piece on emotional resilience and Alice Boyes's chapter on letting go of perfectionism are more relevant than ever—and

I'll be rereading them when we're all back to normal and the business trips, summer camps, and piano practices that come along with it. The advice and encouragement you'll find here are truly evergreen. Of course, given the unique contours of your personal and professional life, you'll latch onto some of these ideas more than others. And you may even disagree with some. That's fine: This book provides you options, and *you* decide which ones to follow through on.

As you read, I encourage you to skim, to jump from one essay to the next, and to do so with a pencil or note-taking app at hand. Jot down the tips and tricks that could have the most impact on keeping you happy, whole, and together both as a professional and as a parent. Then, take that big step forward and allow yourself to *use* them.

Section 1

Give Yourself a Time-Out

Look at How You Spend Your Time

Give Yourself Permission to Recharge

by Elizabeth Grace Saunders

Quick Takes

- Take time for yourself when you need it

- Define what can help you recharge

- Start with 5 or 10 minutes, then go longer

- Work with your partner so you both get the time you need

The arrival of your first child transforms you. All of a sudden, life isn't just about you—or you and your partner. Suddenly a new little life that's 100% dependent on you for absolutely everything has emerged into the world. And you now have the joyous and at times incredibly weighty responsibility to ensure that he or she survives—and hopefully thrives. Over time, this dedication to others around you becomes the norm.

Whether you're a parent to a newborn or a teenager, it's natural, normal, and healthy for your attention to be on your children and to many times put their needs ahead of your own. But many well-meaning parents can shift their focus so much that they completely lose sight of what they need to be happy, healthy people—especially if work is also in the mix. This lack of self-care can lead to parental burnout, which in turn can lead to exceptionally poor parenting, ranging from aggressive to neglectful, and can cause individuals to mentally "check out" at home and potentially at work.

To love and care for your children well, you need to love and care for yourself well. As a time management coach who works with many parents, here are some steps that I've found can lead you in the right direction.

Emphasize the Quality of Your Time

How much time you spend with your children does matter. And it makes sense that if you have limited time with your children that you would want to maximize it. But spending all of your time with your kids when you're not working or sleeping can lead to you being physically present, but mentally and emotionally distant. It's better for you to take some time on your own to be introverted, exercise, or talk with your spouse or a friend, and then come back to your children fully ready to engage than it is to be with your kids longer with your eyes glued to the phone, TV, or laptop, or simply glazed over because you're mentally checked out.

One of the biggest gifts you can give your children is to know that they're a joy to you—that you see them, know them, and are happy to be with them. That happens when you light up when they enter the room, emphasize eye contact, and notice and appreciate what they're doing. Whether they're building with blocks, running around the park, playing sports, or participating in a debate competition, your kids are always glancing back at you and their eyes are asking the questions, "Do you see me? Did you notice me? Do you care? Are you proud of me?"

You can't give them this wholehearted affirmation if you're burned out and trying to take a break from them while they're still there. Allow yourself to take some time for yourself, so you can be fully present.

Define What You Need

Once you've come to some level of acceptance that it's OK to take care of yourself, it's important to define what exactly would help you recharge. Here are a few common self-care areas I've seen for parents:

- Exercise

- Naps

- Time in nature

- Reading

- Time with spouse or partner

- Time with friends

- Alone time, especially for introverts

- Decluttering time

- Prayer

- Journaling

- Artistic expression

Identify simple day-to-day activities that help you feel refreshed so that you're ready to be present for your children when you are with them. Ideally, some of these items can become a regular part of your lifestyle so that you consistently refill your energy tank before it gets too low.

Start with Small Shifts— and Then Go Longer

If you feel exceptionally strapped for time, begin with micro-changes to carve out regular time for yourself. That could be even 5 to 10 minutes at the beginning of the day to stretch, pray, meditate, or do anything else that centers you. It could mean taking 10 minutes at lunch to read a book. Or taking a quick walk in the afternoon to refresh physically and mentally. When I have a tight schedule, I'll take a 5-minute walk where I just go up and down the block. Even that small bit of physical activity outside can make a measurable difference in mental health.

Challenge yourself to find bits of time throughout your day for small activities that nourish you. That email can wait—and so can the dishes. By taking truly satisfying breaks throughout your day, you'll reduce the need to zone out in the evening.

As you take more and more micro-breaks, you may discover that you can carve out longer periods of time to devote to self-care. To ensure commitment, you may need to incorporate some outside accountability. That could be working out with a trainer, signing up for an exercise class, joining a team, planning to meet up with a friend, or participating in a book club. Committing to activities with others that reinforce the positive investments you want to make in yourself can help you to follow through when you're tempted to put your needs aside.

Look for Special Opportunities

Most of the time, you'll be investing in smaller bits of self-care throughout your days. But on occasion, you may have the opportunity for larger blocks of time to recharge. If possible, take them. If you have family that is able and willing to care for your children, consider a weekend getaway every once in a while. Or add an extra day on to your business travel so you can get some refresh time. Look for Parents Night Out events at places like the YMCA or churches where for a small fee (or sometimes for free), your children can have a fun time with other kids and you can get a break. Or even arrange to work at home some days to have time alone in your home.

These opportunities can help you shift out of feeling as if you never get a break and help you come back to your family responsibilities with renewed energy.

Support Your Spouse or Partner

If you have a spouse or partner, work together to support one another in having time to recharge. When you work together to give one another time off, you can avoid either one of you burning out on your parenting duties. This will not only help you parent better, but also help you have a happier, healthier relationship. (Chapter 8 will help you conduct these conversations.)

I've seen coaching clients work together with their spouses or partners in many different ways to take care of the kids so they each could have some extra time away. In one case, my coaching client had Monday night to practice with his band, and his wife had Wednesday night for horseback-riding lessons. Another couple had different nights that they spent with their friend groups: The wife had a girls' night once a week, and the husband had a night with the guys once a week. Another couple switched off when they took responsibility for morning duty so that they each had some mornings where they could go into the office or work out early. Finally, another had a babysitter come for a few hours on the weekend, so they could have time as a couple or accomplish personal tasks without having full responsibility for the kids.

Could you spend more time with your kids? Definitely. But will you look back and regret it if you went through your kids' childhood being grumpy and surviving on fumes? For sure. Your children want and need you to be joyful and connected with yourself so that you can connect with them in joyful ways. Give yourself permission to take care of yourself, so you can better take care of your kids.

Adapted from "Working Parents, Give Yourself Permission to Recharge," on hbr.org, February 24, 2020 (product #H05FYR).

Working Dads Need "Me Time," Too

by Alyssa F. Westring and Stewart D. Friedman

Quick Takes

- Beware of dropping everything that isn't work or family
- Create experiments to fold self-care into your schedule
- Focus on rejuvenating and restoring activities
- Accept that you may struggle at first

Mother's Day is widely recognized as a day to acknowledge moms who all too often forsake relaxation and self-care for family, work, and community responsibilities. It's no surprise that many Mother's Day gifts are designed to give Mom one day to put herself first—like sleeping in, taking a break from chores and cooking, or getting a massage or pedicure, for example. Yet, few people acknowledge the fact that dads, too, are now increasingly engaged in childcare and household responsibilities, in addition to demanding jobs.

Fathers report levels of work-family conflict on par with (and, in some cases, higher than) mothers.[1] In addition, fathers who give higher-than-average levels of childcare, ask for paternity leave, or interrupt their careers for family reasons are harassed more at work, receive worse performance evaluations, and get paid less than men who either don't have kids or don't spend much time with them. And when fathers ask for flex-time, they're often even more penalized than mothers are for making the same request.[2]

We need to recognize that working fathers, like working mothers, are susceptible to the "putting everyone else first" challenge of modern working-parenthood. We're already seeing this start to happen, and this increased visibility will hopefully lead to the systemic interventions we know work best. But in the meantime, how can individual dads start solving the problem of work-life conflict?

We set out to study working fathers of young children in our Total Leadership program—a widely recognized leadership development program that focuses on integrating four areas of life (work, home, community, and self) for improved performance in all four. The process starts with each participant diagnosing what matters most to him and engaging in dialogues with key stakeholders (spouse, boss, kids, and so on). Each participant then experiments with new ways of getting things done that serve all the different parts of their lives; they pursue "four-way wins."

We conducted an in-depth analysis of 36 working fathers of young children (under age three) who participated in this program as part of their Wharton Executive MBA. At the beginning of the program, it was clear that these fathers were skipping sleep, exercise, healthy eating, spiritual growth, and relaxation for the sake of their work and family responsibilities. Indeed, at the start of the experiment, they rated their satisfaction with their personal well-being as an average of 4.3 on a scale from 1 (not at all satisfied) to 10 (fully satisfied). This is in contrast to their reported satisfaction with work and with family, which were both rated significantly higher, with averages of 7.4 and 6.5, respectively. In other words, they were putting everyone else first—and themselves last.

So it wasn't surprising that when asked to design experiments to enhance performance in all areas of their lives, the most popular type of experiment for these new dads was "rejuvenating and restoring" (as compared to, say, planning or time-shifting). R&Rs involve taking care of yourself (for example, changes in diet or physical activity, doing meditation, taking vacation, etc.) to increase capacity and performance at work, in your family, and in the community via positive spillover—indirect effects that ripple out from the self to other parts of life. In an earlier study of the nine kinds of experiments, 57% of program participants completed an R&R. However, 75% of those in our working fathers sample did so, indicating a greater need for this sort of change in their lives.[3]

After their conversations with key stakeholders and some intensive coaching, the fathers in our sample implemented their experiments over the course of the subsequent 12 to 15 weeks. One decided to do yoga for three hours each week, with the expectation that it would "improve my physical fitness, mental concentration at work and school, outward confidence, and show importance of exercise to my kids and other stakeholders." Another committed to "exercise three times regularly a week because this will allow me to have more energy at home for the limited time I have for my wife and kids, providing me with the energy at work to handle stress better, be more patient, and be a much better leader ... it will allow me to regain the health and peace of mind I so desperately need for myself."

The goal is not for participants to implement their experiments perfectly, exactly as designed. Instead, the purpose is to gain experience with trying new ways of doing things and thereby increase one's confidence and competence in one's capacity to initiate change that's truly sustainable. We were not surprised to find that many participants struggled to implement their well-being initiatives exactly as designed, given the intensive demands of their work, school, and family responsibilities.

Yet, even for those who struggled to fully follow through on attending anew to their personal needs as they had mapped out in the designs for their experiments, there was much growth and an increase in optimism. For instance, one father wrote that "this experiment and the introspection I have gained has taught me that without a healthy 'you' it is very difficult to excel or be your very best in other areas." Another wrote, "Giving time to oneself is very important. In our daily lives which have become so wired and busy, we hardly do that. Exercise and diet is just one of the ways to achieve that." Just as with working moms, several of the dads noted the importance of caring for oneself as a foundation for caring for others.

One father aptly wrote, that "I heard someone refer to this as the analogy of putting on the oxygen mask before helping others, and that is how I feel."

At the conclusion of our program, we asked participants to again rate their satisfaction with the different areas of their lives. Working fathers' satisfaction with the "self" domain improved from 4.3 to an average of 6.5, a statistically significant increase. And these gains in the personal domain were not accomplished at the cost of reduced satisfaction in other domains. Significant increases were also observed, as satisfaction with work and family also rose, to an average of 8.4 and 8.5, respectively (see figure 2-1). On separate measures, participants also reported significant improvements in physical health and mental health, as well as a reduction in stress.

FIGURE 2-1

Taking care of yourself doesn't mean letting others down

Working dads who consciously took more time for themselves for 12–15 weeks felt better about their personal well-being—and their work and families.

	Satisfied with personal well-being	Satisfied with work	Satisfied with family
Before taking time for self	4.3	7.4	6.5
After taking time for self	6.5	8.4	8.5

Scale: 1 = Not at all satisfied; 10 = Fully satisfied

All of us fall into the trap of saying we can't afford to take time for ourselves; what's important about our study is that it shows that on the contrary, we *have* to take time for ourselves in order to effectively serve others. It isn't only moms who tend to put themselves at the bottom of the list, nor is it only mothers who can benefit from more self-care. Today's fathers need it, too.

Adapted from content posted on hbr.org, June 13, 2014 (product #H00UY3).

Does Your Schedule Reflect Your Values?

by Elizabeth Grace Saunders

Quick Takes

- Use a values-driven schedule to be more intentional with your time
- Decide what's important—and what isn't
- Define *why* what's important matters to you
- Identify related actions and put them in your calendar
- Discuss your schedule with those who may be impacted

A very wise friend once told me, "Talking about parenting is like talking about politics." She's right.

Because of the highly personal nature of parenting, individuals tend to have strong opinions of the way things "should" be as a working parent. Being pulled in different directions—the expectations from both work and home, and the stress that comes with them—can mean parents struggle with questions like: Can I make it home in time for dinner? Will I be able to help with evening activities? Will work be done in time for me to tuck my kids into bed? How much travel is too much? Should I take time during the day to exercise if it means I don't see the kids before school or I get home later? Is it OK for me to see my friends if I feel like I barely get enough time with my family?

As a time management coach, my role is not to critique your parenting style but to encourage you to live a life aligned with your values. Especially as a working parent, that requires you to be exceptionally intentional with your time. Part of that is developing—and living by—a values-driven schedule. A values-driven schedule requires you to determine what is most important to you and your family, and then craft your calendar around those priorities, rather than fitting your family and yourself in around whatever might land on your plate. This helps ensure that you can feel overall satisfied with your time and parenting choices, instead of feeling guilty or frustrated that you're not investing your time in the people and activities that matter most to you.

Here is a three-step process to create a values-driven schedule, based on strategies I've seen be effective for my clients who are working parents. Table 3-1 offers you a sample worksheet to use for this exercise.

Step 1: Get Clear on What's Most Important

Begin by listing these key items:

- **The categories you want to include in your schedule.** Consider time for work, family, exercise, learning, social activities, alone time, hobbies, etc.

- **The level of achievement you want in these areas.** Identify your goals and the time commitment required. Going to the gym to work out for 40 minutes three times a week is a different time commitment than training for an Ironman, just as making time to see some of your child's soccer

TABLE 3-1

The values-driven schedule worksheet

	Step 1: Goals/routines	Time	Step 2: Why
Family			
Work			
Exercise			
Social activities			
Hobbies			
[enter personal goal]			

games requires less time than coaching the team. Be realistic about how much time you'll need for each category you've written down.

- **Essential rituals for yourself or your family.** Maybe you want to be home for family dinner at least three nights a week, attend a service at a place of worship each week, and detach from electronics by 10 p.m. so you can connect with your spouse or partner before bed. Jot these routines down and how regularly they should happen.

Your time choices impact not only you but also the other members of your family. As you make this list, have some discussions with your kids and spouse or co-parent about what matters most to them. For example, maybe your son doesn't mind you heading to the office before he gets up, but it would mean the world to him if you leave work in time to see him in his school play.

This is also a really good time to identify what's *not* important for you to do. Perhaps there are professional organizations where membership would be nice but the decreased time with your family isn't worth the trade-off right now. Or you may have the ability to get outside help with some tasks such as housecleaning, lawn care, errands, or handyman items, so you can use that time working on your side gig or spending time with your kids.

Step 2: Define Why They're Important

Once you have defined your categories, levels of achievement, and essential rituals, think of *why* each one of these is important to you. Go through each one and write down why you believe they are significant.

Thinking about the "why" can strengthen your resolve to follow through. It's one thing to say, "I should exercise," but it's another to frame it as, "I want to exercise because I want to live a long, healthy life where I can be present for my children and my future grandchildren." It can also help you weed out false priorities. For instance, if the strongest reason you can think of for taking a job that will mean 50%–75% travel is that it's the usual next step in your career path, step back and think again. Would you love that job? Would it help you fulfill your potential? Would it match your goals? If so, go for it. But if it's just what people usually do but you're not that excited about it, seriously consider whether it's worth that much time away from your family. We often have more options than we think in our jobs, and success comes in many forms.

As you evaluate the "why," look at everything from a 50-year point of view. Think about what you wrote down and ask yourself, "Fifty years from now, what choices would I have been happy that I made? What would matter to me? What wouldn't?" In the moment, things like a work contract can seem so incredibly urgent and important, but over the 50-year span, making (or missing) memories with your family will likely be what you remember.

Step 3: Fuse Your Priorities with Your Schedule

Once you're clear on your priorities, identify related actions and put them in your calendar. This helps to make doing them more automatic and makes it much easier to live a values-driven life.

Start by plugging your essential rituals into your calendar, and then add new items as recurring events based on your priorities. Here are some examples of priorities translated into calendar actions:

- **Exercise.** Go to the gym on Monday, Wednesday, and Friday before work from 6:30 to 7:30 a.m.

- **Family time.** Eat breakfast with the family on Saturday mornings around 8 a.m.

- **Connection time.** For 15–20 minutes before their bedtime, talk to the kids about anything on their minds. Spend some time talking with my spouse before going to bed as well.

- **Activity time.** Leave at 4:30 p.m. on Tuesdays to take my daughter to dance class.

- **Alone time:** Take a 15-minute walk around 2:30 p.m. to clear my head and get refreshed.

Then have discussions with the people who this might impact about how you can make this work for all of you—and why it's so important. Maybe your spouse or partner helps get the kids ready on the mornings you work out. Then you return the favor the other days. With your children, there may be days when you need to work late to make up the time you took off to take your child to dance class or to participate in another extracurricular activity. But if you explain to them that you want to make time to talk before bed and really follow through on that commitment, that can help them still feel heard and connected. And if your values-based schedule adjustments impact your normal working hours, you may also want to have a discussion with your boss to explain your intentions.

The needs of each family are unique, but the importance of values-based scheduling is universal. Take the time to think through these three steps and create a schedule that reflects your priorities and values, so that you'll look back with satisfaction on the choices you made as a working parent.

Adapted from "Working Parents: Does Your Schedule Reflect Your Values?" on hbr.org, November 26, 2019 (product #H05AMY).

Six Ways to Weave Self-Care into Your Workday

by Amy Jen Su

Quick Takes

- Realize you can be your own harshest critic

- Jot down key priorities each day

- Celebrate your successes

- Surround yourself with people who support you

- Make your workspace a reflection of your best self

- Stay attuned to your energy levels and recharge

've spent the past few years working closely with leaders on incorporating self-care into their work lives—as a key component of their overall performance—so that an expansion in their role or responsibilities doesn't come at the expense of their health and well-being. One CEO I worked with summed it up best when he said, "Self-care is no longer a luxury; it's part of the job."

So, what exactly *is* self-care, and how do we do it?

Define Self-Care More Broadly

At the heart of self-care is your relationship and connection to self. As part of your job, it means that you're attuned to and understand what you need to be your most constructive, effective, and authentic self. Therefore, rather than narrowly defining self-care as just physical health (which is an important piece of the equation), you need to pay attention to a wider set of criteria, including care of the mind, emotions, relationships, environment, time, and resources.

Take Out the Word "Should"

Self-care can feel daunting or unattainable. But the intention is not to add more to your already full plate, or create a reason to beat yourself up. For example, you might find yourself annoyed when someone suggests that you need to take better care of yourself, especially when it seems they don't understand how much you've already got on your plate. Self-care doesn't originate from judgment and isn't reactive to judgment (both are forms of self-sabotage, as I describe later). Instead, self-care flows from an intention to stay connected to oneself and one's overall mission: *Who and what can support and be in service of the positive contribution I hope to make?*

Operationalize Self-Care in Your Day-to-Day Work

Rather than having self-care be something outside of work, it's important to weave it naturally into the course of your workday. Below are six ways I've seen clients take purposeful action. Self-care is highly personal, though, so rather than being an exhaustive list, these ideas are meant to get your gears turning:

Cut yourself a break

We can often be our own harshest critic. When the weight of accountability or perfectionism kicks in, ask yourself: "What would I say to a colleague or friend in the same situation?" Research from Harvard Business School professor Amy Edmondson has shown that we optimize performance and learning in groups when both accountability and psychological safety are present.[1] These principles can also help you as an individual. By keeping your internal critic at bay, you can create the right psychological conditions to accelerate through periods of rumination or self-doubt more quickly.

Value time, money, and resources

Throughout a given workday, others frequently ask for our time or resources, distracting us from more important priorities. That's why it's important to set aside 15 minutes first thing each morning to jot down the three things you hope to accomplish that day. Then, as requests come in, consider the impact on your priorities before offering a knee-jerk, automatic yes. For those who are self-employed, the same goes when you are asked about your fees and services. Self-care means honoring the value, impact, and contribution you bring.

Take a victory lap

What did you do last week? Most of us can't remember because once we've completed a deliverable or gotten through a tough crunch, we've already moved on to the next thing. Instead, hit the pause button with yourself and your team to take a look back at the previous month or quarter, and name or write down what went well or what felt particularly satisfying. This kind of debrief can help you and your team stay connected to passions, highest contributions, and actions that actually add value.

Surround yourself with good people

Healthy and supportive relationships are a critical part of self-care. Consider whether your team is providing ample leverage and support to meet priorities. Take notice of who feeds your energy and who drains it. Set more boundaries with the drainers. Invest in those who inspire and support you and who understand what it means to have a healthy give-and-take. The same goes for your relationships outside of work. Don't let work cause you to neglect the most important people in your life. Use breaks during the day, or perhaps your commute time, to call friends and loved ones, and carve out plenty of time outside of work to nurture relationships.

Update your workspace

Our environment and workspace can have a significant impact on productivity. Gain more mental clarity by cleaning up your desk. Put up pictures, artwork, or images that inspire you or remind you of the people and things that matter. Your workspace should feel like a reflection of your best self.

Recharge and reboot

Stay attuned to your energy levels. For most busy professionals, getting eight hours of sleep every night is (sadly) not realistic. But it's important to at least try to refill your gas tank during the week, so designate a Wednesday or Thursday night to get in some extra sleep. And it's equally important to build restoration breaks into your workday. For example, try scheduling more walking meetings, or make a point of having lunch away from your desk with a colleague or friend. If you're traveling for work and find yourself with an extra 30 minutes before boarding a flight, stop by one of the airport massage stands to relax and recharge before your trip.

Notice When You've Slipped Out of Self-Care Mode

In times of stress, self-care can get especially off-balance. Be aware, with self-compassion, of when you've lost touch with your authentic self in one of the following ways.

Self-neglect

With demanding workloads and overly full plates, self-neglect can become a familiar pattern for many of us. It feels like we're always running on a hamster wheel. As feelings of anxiety and being overwhelmed increase, it becomes harder to maintain composure and say no to the daily fire drills, interruptions, and demands of others. We end our workdays feeling completely burned out.

Self-management

Maintaining a professional and competent persona is an important leadership skill, but in some cases, we can take it too far. When you spend too much energy managing how you come across to other people or putting on your best face all the time, you suppress or deny emotion, working hard to uphold a professional game face. You end up feeling exhausted from keeping up the act, and risk being perceived as inauthentic.

Self-sabotage

Sometimes, we don't achieve our mission or highest priorities because we have gotten in our own way. Notice when you have slipped into unproductive habits of procrastination, rumination, or distraction to avoid the anxiety or fear of completing your most important tasks.

Self-preservation

In a competitive world, it's easy to succumb to a scarcity mindset. When we're overly focused on a lack of resources, we can lose touch with what's best for the business. Being overly competitive can cause others to perceive you as protecting your own turf and being in it for yourself.

In each of these cases, we are no longer in the driver's seat. Instead, anxiety, control, disdain of vulnerability, or fear is running the show. Notice, without judgment, when you've slipped into one of these places, and then gently reach for a self-care action to come back to yourself more fully.

Adapted from content posted on hbr.org, June 19, 2017 (product #H03QHM).

Do More by Doing Less (at Home and at Work)

by Kate Northrup

Quick Takes

- Pick an area of your life you want to improve

- List the tasks and activities you do in that area

- Write down your biggest wins in that area

- Circle the activities that were most responsible for your wins

- Cut back on everything else

W e've been taught that if we want more—money, achievement, vitality, joy, peace of mind—we need to *do* more, to add more to our ever-growing to-do list. But what if we've been taught wrong? What if the answer to getting more of what we want isn't addition at all, but subtraction?

As it turns out, evidence supports that if we want to ramp up our productivity and happiness, we should actually be doing less. David Rock, author of *Your Brain at Work*, found that we're truly focused on our work a mere 6 hours *per week*, which starkly contrasts with our collective buy-in to the 40-hour workweek. When you stop doing the things that make you feel busy but aren't getting you results (and are draining you of energy), then you end up with more than enough time for what matters and a sense of peace and spaciousness that constant activity has kept outside your reach.

As people with full lives—kids, careers, friends, passions, logistics, and more—how can we apply the wisdom of doing less to give ourselves more time and alleviate stress without jeopardizing our results?

We need to identify what *not* to do. But this determination can't be random. It must be methodical and evidence-based. Through my work with women navigating the dual vocations of entrepreneurship and motherhood, I've created a surprisingly simple exercise to help individuals decide what activities on their to-do list bring them the most value, and which they can stop doing. Here's how it works:

Step 1. Draw a line down the middle of a piece of paper, lengthwise.

Step 2. Decide on an area of your life or work where you'd like to have better results and less stress. For example, perhaps you want to expand your thought leadership.

Step 3. On the left-hand side, list the tasks or activities you do in that area of your work or life. As an aspiring thought leader, you might list attending conferences, pitching organizations for speaking opportunities, writing new articles, reading and researching, and so on.

Step 4. On the right-hand side, make a list of your biggest wins in that area, like a speaking gig, a presentation you really nailed at work, or a pitch that was accepted at a major publication. This can often be a difficult step for some people. We have not been culturally conditioned to celebrate ourselves, so folks will often draw a blank when listing their wins. Any result you've gotten (either one time or repeatedly) that was positive can go on this list. Don't get caught up in listing the "right" things. Just list what comes to you.

Step 5. Draw a line connecting each of your biggest wins to the activity or task that was most responsible for that result. Reading and researching, for instance, were essential to getting your pitch accepted for publication, so connect these two together.

Step 6. Circle all the activities and tasks on the left side of your paper that have been responsible for your big wins. Look at what's left. Whatever isn't circled is something that you need to stop doing completely, significantly minimize, or delegate if it absolutely must be done. For instance, if you discover that traveling for conferences once a month isn't directly contributing to any wins, it's time to set that aside or at least cut back.

This same approach can be used to determine where to do less in other areas of your life. For instance, if you're looking to connect more with your children, you might list a few specific memories or wins when you really felt as if you were being the best parent you could be, such as singing silly songs with your preschooler while folding the laundry on a Sunday morning or when your preteen bared their soul to you and you felt so honored by how safe they felt to tell you the hard stuff.

Now think about the tasks you do on a regular basis: laundry, making lunch, reminding your kids to do their schoolwork, checking off committee items for the PTA, planning play dates (even virtually), making sure everyone has clothes that fit, scheduling pediatrician appointments, and so on. While these tasks may need to be done, this exercise can give us permission to spend less time on these activities. Often the things we think we must do are simply because we always have done them or others around us do them and we think we should, too. Such a perspective creates unnecessary stress when we do these tasks late, make errors, or ask for help. Maybe instead of serving on the PTA, you can just attend the occasional meeting—or follow up with another parent who regularly attends. Perhaps you can set up a system where your children are in charge of making sure their schoolwork is done by a particular time each day, rather than reminding them yourself. On the other hand, if you discover that making lunch with your preteen provided that opportunity for them to initiate a heart-to-heart, maybe that's something you'd like to keep on your list. (Figure 5-1 illustrates more of this exercise and these connections.)

Repeat this exercise for as many areas of your life that you'd like to enhance through subtraction. Be ruthless.

FIGURE 5-1

"Big wins" in parenting

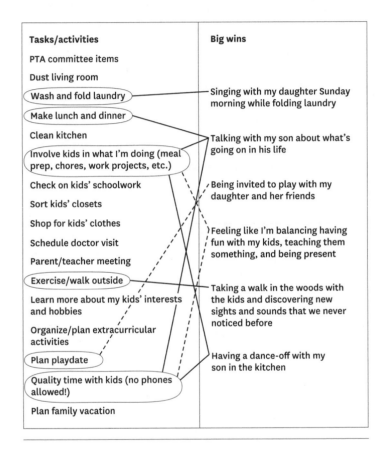

And don't forget to consider what brings you joy. Not only does happiness make you at least 12% more productive, it's also what makes life worth living in the first place.[1] Activities where you're focusing on yourself—through meditation or exercise—can lead to wins, simply because they allow you to be more present or calm in the moment.

Life is not about racking up a list of accomplishments. What can you stop doing to make more time for yourself, make more time for joy, and use your time more meaningfully? The next time you set a goal or decide you want to improve upon an area of your life—or simply alleviate some of the pain that area is causing you—remember to go for subtraction instead of addition. Revel in the joy of doing less.

Adapted from "Want to Be More Productive? Try Doing Less," on hbr.org, May 21, 2020 (product #H05MGT).

Section 2

Learn to Talk

Communicate Your Needs

Four Conversations Every Overwhelmed Working Parent Should Have

by Joseph Grenny and Brittney Maxfield

Quick Takes

- Ask yourself who you are and what you want

- Talk about your career and family commitments with your boss and colleagues

- Define common goals for your children with your spouse or partner

- Open up to your kids about the pressures you feel and what you want

Working parents sometimes struggle with the feeling that they are either letting down their family or not meeting their career goals. It can be hard to strike the right balance. As with most of the challenges we face at work, having an open and honest conversation is one of the first steps toward finding a solution. If you're able to talk about the issue, you can often resolve it, or at least come to a compromise.

One of us, Brittney, became a mom eight years ago and went through this experience of renegotiating boundaries in an intentional way. The other, Joseph, saw how Brittney's skill in doing this not only made Brittney happier but also changed our whole company culture to be more supportive of working parents.

If you are a parent looking to establish and sustain a healthier balance—for yourself, your children, and even your organization—there are four specific types of conversations we recommend having.

A Conversation with Yourself

The first ongoing conversation you need to have is with yourself. You must clarify who you are and what you want before you can confidently negotiate your boundaries. If you fail to hold this initial conversation, emotion can override reason, and it's easy to get caught up in an unwinnable game of pleasing someone else rather than choosing what is right for you. Having this conversation with yourself first will make all the other conversations less stressful.

A Conversation with Your Boss and Colleagues

View this as an ongoing tactical conversation in which you negotiate the specifics of your schedule and workload.

Sit down with your boss and teammates and let them know of your passion for your career and your work-related goals, and then unapologetically share how your family commitments relate to these priorities. For example, you might say, "I want to manage large projects. I'm at my best when I'm getting important things done. I'm willing to sprint for short periods of time to ensure that everything works, but these sprints will have to be occasional. I also intend to be a consistent presence in my children's lives." Having laid out these principles frankly, check to see if your colleagues are expressing mild disappointment, support, or simply concession. If they buy in grudgingly, you should expect worse when your boundaries cost them in specific ways.

It's possible that your teammates won't support the life you are committed to creating for yourself. But remember—even if this conversation goes poorly, you haven't failed. Knowing where everybody stands will provide you with the information you need to make the best choice about how to move forward with your career. You might determine that leaving the organization and finding a more supportive company is the best way for you to reach your goals and avoid the alternative: a slow, inexorable path to separation.

When Brittney returned to work, she was initially nervous about asking her manager for more flexibility and a slightly reduced schedule, which she felt she needed in order to have more time at home. Ultimately, their conversation was successful because she strongly believed that a more flexible schedule would allow her to better meet her obligations at home *and* at the office.

A Conversation with Your Partner or Spouse

Speak honestly with your partner or spouse about your common goals for your children. If, for example, you both agree that it's essential for at least one parent to be present at important events in your child's life, then find ways to tag-team these commitments. You may be willing to speak to your boss about your work-life balance goals, but if your partner isn't willing to do the same, it will be challenging to meet the goals you set and the two of you may fall into mutual resentment. Encourage your partner to hold these difficult conversations at their workplace so that together you can accomplish your goals.

When Brittney adjusted her work schedule, her self-employed husband made similar sacrifices. Though he was working tirelessly to get a business off the ground, he reduced his schedule to spend time with their son while Brittney was at the office—and vice versa. This teamwork approach helped them manage their time in ways that aligned with their goals.

A Conversation with Your Child(ren)

When your children are old enough to understand, talk frankly with them about the pressures you feel and what you truly want. However, be careful to avoid playing the role of the victim. Blaming your organization for your lack of flexibility or stress at home doesn't solve problems; it creates unfair and false resentments. The last thing you want to do is teach your children to despise the idea of work. Instead, model by example.

Acknowledge all the commitments you've willingly made both at work and at home. Help your children understand the time you spend away from them isn't just that—time away. It's something you value that also contributes to a happier life at home for the whole family. Talk to your kids about your passion for your work, the skills you've developed to excel at your position, and how it brings you joy. Explain how much you want to put them first and that when you can't, it's hard on you, too. Don't brush off difficult feelings. Own the sadness you might feel when you can't be there. Feeling sad together actually creates connection. If your child sees that it's hard for you, they can better understand that your occasional absence is no reflection of your love for them.

When Brittney was required to travel for her job, she never pretended that she was being forced to leave by a sinister boss, even if that would've been an easier message to deliver to her kids. She told her boys she would miss them but that, right now, she had to fulfill other important responsibilities. Now that her children are older, she talks honestly with them about schedules and priorities. In these ongoing conversations, she explains that even when Mom and Dad are busy with work, the family's needs are always the top priority.

There's no denying these four conversations are challenging to have and may not always go as well as you planned, depending on your circumstances and the expectations of your boss, coworkers, and partner. Having them also doesn't guarantee that your career won't be at all affected, especially if you're a woman. Unfortunately, we still live in a world where too many women experience a motherhood penalty of reduced opportunity and compensation in their careers. Having the four conversations does not guarantee inoculation against these workplace inequities, but it *does* guarantee the *possibility* of achieving the change you want to see in your life. If you never have the conversation, you fail before you try.

Balance is a never-ending pursuit that requires constant awareness and communication—but with skill and purpose, it can be done. And as a parent, what better motivation to establish and sustain a healthy work-life balance than our children?

Adapted from content posted on hbr.org, August 8, 2018 (product #H04GAT).

What's a Working Dad to Do?

by Scott Behson

Quick Takes

- Own your role in changing the conversation about working fathers
- Talk about your family at work and ask other men about theirs
- Start an informal group to discuss your lives outside of work
- Use work flexibility—and ensure that others see you doing it
- Take your full paternity leave, so others will model your behavior

was once on a radio show to discuss the struggles men face in trying to balance work and family demands. During the interview, the cohost told a quick anecdote about a run-in he had when he was a rising corporate lawyer at a prestigious New York City firm.

He was divorced and his ex-wife and his kids lived in London, so he flew there to see his kids every other weekend. After two monster weeks of work, he was heading out of the office to go to JFK airport late one Thursday afternoon when a more senior partner confronted him, saying, "Where are you going?"

The cohost responded, explaining that he'd bulked up the past two weeks to finish his work for his very satisfied client and that he was catching his flight to Heathrow to see his kids. The partner angrily responded, "Bullshit. You see your kids more than I do, and I live with mine. Besides I need you here tonight—and over the weekend." The cohost pushed back and caught his flight, but shortly thereafter decided to give up his career as a lawyer. Life was just too short.

This is an extreme example, but many working fathers face similar pressures to conform to a traditional gender role that insists they be "all in" for work, regardless of achievement level and regardless of family responsibilities. And this is the case despite the facts that:

- Dual-income, shared-care families are far more the norm than families with a single-earner and an at-home spouse.

- Today's fathers spend three times as much time with their children and twice as much time on housework than dads did a generation ago.

- Men aspire to be even more involved in their families than they are.[1]

As a result, it has been reported that dads experience at least as much work-family conflict as mothers, and that in some ways, men are facing a funhouse-mirror version of women's struggles to attain success at both work and home.[2]

A few years ago, the Flexibility Stigma Working Group at The Center for WorkLife Law at the UC Hastings College of the Law, consisting of researchers from over a dozen universities, published a series of research studies in a special issue of the *Journal of Social Issues* entitled "The Flexibility Stigma." About half of the articles focus on barriers men face in the workplace as they try to balance work and family demands. Among their findings:

- While men value work flexibility, they are reluctant to seek out flexible work arrangements because of fears of being seen as uncommitted and unmanly, and expectations of potential career consequences. These fears, unfortunately, prove to be well founded.

- Fathers who engage in higher-than-average levels of childcare are subject to more workplace harassment (for example, picked on for "not being man enough") and more general mistreatment (for example, garden-variety workplace aggression) as compared to their low-caregiving or childless counterparts.

- Men requesting family leave are perceived as uncommitted to work and less masculine; these perceptions are linked to lower performance evaluations, increased risks of being demoted or downsized, and reduced pay and rewards.

- Finally, men who interrupt their employment for family reasons earn significantly less after returning to work.

All in all, that's a pretty stark set of findings. What's a working father to do? The first step toward healthier workplace culture is to bring the fathers' work-family issue out of the shadows and to make it a topic for discussion—and that starts with fathers themselves.

As Gandhi said, "We need to be the change we wish to see." If you have the security, flexibility, courage, and inclination (I recognize some may have more ability to do this at work than others), here are four things working dads can do in our workplaces to make it easier for all of us to discuss and address our work-family concerns.

- While at work, talk about your family and ask other men about theirs.

- Reach out to some male work friends and start an informal group to discuss your lives outside of work. Have lunch together or grab a drink after work and talk.

- Use work flexibility and let your male colleagues see you do so. Tell people you are leaving early for a school event but are taking work home. Or, explain why working from home a few days a week is so valuable, since you're able to replace commuting time with helping your kids with their schoolwork.

- At the birth of a new child, take your full paternity leave. Make a plan and communicate it to others in your company, signaling your commitment as a dedicated father and employee. (As a leader or manager, this is especially important, as others will model your behavior.)

We need to make it more normal for working fathers to discuss and address family issues. I know it is not easy to stand out. But these small steps can lay the groundwork for communicating your needs as a parent and building more supportive workplace cultures.

Adapted from content posted on hbr.org, August 21, 2013.

How to Communicate Your Self-Care Needs to Your Partner

by Jackie Coleman

Quick Takes

- Find a time to talk that is free of distractions and relatively calm

- Use "I feel" statements to avoid blame or criticism

- Listen actively—and be willing to compromise

- Do regular checkups on your relationship and family

The morning rush: shower, eat breakfast, get the kids dressed, start the day. The workday: meetings, then calls, then more meetings. The evening: dinner, baths, bedtimes. Climb into bed, only to start over again. Lather, rinse, repeat.

As a working parent with a seemingly endless array of responsibilities, it can be hard to make space for yourself. The tendency to focus all your energy on work or family and put your own needs on hold is the norm. And extreme or unusual circumstances—like the recent Covid pandemic—can only make this more difficult. As parents and children found themselves stuck at home juggling work, school, and entertainment, it felt as if there was even less time to dedicate to their own needs.

But the benefits of taking care of yourself, whether that's physically, emotionally, spiritually, or mentally, are undeniable. It's the whole "adjust your oxygen mask first before assisting another" principle. My husband, John, and I call it creating a "third space"—space outside of home and work to explore interests, decompress, and find personal fulfillment. This can lead to decreased anxiety, increased productivity, and overall higher levels of life satisfaction.

But even when you know the benefits of focusing on your own physical and mental health, it can be challenging to communicate your personal needs to your partner. Feelings of guilt or shame may prevent these conversations, but not sharing your feelings and needs can lead to resentment, exhaustion, and contempt. And failing to reserve time for yourself can make you less happy and less effective both at work and at home.

So how can you better communicate to your partner a need for a third space or personal time? As a wife, mother of three, and former marriage counselor who has worked with numerous couples, I see a few distinct ways.

First, know what you need. Take two minutes right now to list what third space would most benefit you. Jot down whatever comes to mind. The stereotypical picture of self-care is a vision of someone lounging in a white bathrobe with cucumbers over their eyes. And while some spa time can be great relaxation for some people, there are so many other possibilities. Is it taking 15 minutes after work to sit and decompress before jumping in to help with the kids? Maybe it's enjoying a couple of hours on a weeknight or weekend to read a book for fun. Research has found that simply anticipating an activity or event has many benefits.[1] So maybe you don't need weekly time but would enjoy having something big to look forward to, like a future weekend away with friends or a night alone in a hotel. I have personally taken up guitar and voice lessons, which at first seemed self-indulgent (read:

Create a Third Space

by Jackie Coleman and John Coleman

When professionals have families, their entire lives can revolve around their responsibilities at work and at home. Busy executives run home to help with kids (changing diapers or shuttling preteens to soccer games) or to do the little things that keep a home humming, like laundry, yard work, or cooking. But having a third space outside of work and home can help enormously with stress management.

Each partner in a relationship should maintain habits and times that allow them to explore their interests, relax and seek fulfillment, and find space outside of home and work. These spaces are different for everyone—quiet cafés, virtual book clubs, trout streams, karate classes, poker nights—but they are important for maintaining our identities and our sense of peace.

Make the sacrifice of offering your partner a third space to find themselves, maintain their friendships, and explore their interests, and ask that they do the same for you. This may mean taking over as solo parent on a regular basis—prepping meals, assisting with schoolwork, even covering bath- and bedtime. Third spaces mean no person runs from responsibility to responsibility without having time to breathe.

Adapted from "Don't Take Work Stress Home with You," posted on hbr.org, July 28, 2016 (product #H0315M).

guilt!) but has quickly become life-giving. Even virtual lessons can offer you the space you need. Look at your list and highlight what sticks out to you the most. Then consider whether the top few choices are feasible for your available time and finances, and whether they'll truly recharge you.

Now that you have thought through your own needs and desires, how do you actually have a successful and productive conversation? Consider these tactical suggestions.

Timing is everything

There are moments during the day when a conversation of substance would fail miserably: the minute your spouse or partner signs off from work or walks in the door, the bath-time rush, and the "witching hour(s)" getting kids fed and ready for bed, to name a few. To avoid this, set aside a time together that is free of distractions, relatively calm, and likely to be when neither of you is overtired. The best approach is to make it fun and think of it not as a way to challenge your partner, but as a way to connect. John and I love grabbing a snack and sitting together by our little pond in the front yard after we finish the kids' bedtimes. These moments are peaceful and never feel onerous. Finding this type of breather provides the right context for a promising conversation.

Remember you're playing for the same team

Approach the conversation in this way: You are your spouse's advocate and supporter, just as they are yours. And you both have one another's health and well-being in mind. John Gottman, a prominent researcher on marital success, encourages a "soft startup." This means handling the conversation with gentleness and avoiding blame or criticism. You can do this by using "I feel" statements that focus on your own thoughts and needs instead of universal and accusatory statements like "You always" or ". . . never," etc. Realize it is much easier to hear, "I am feeling really tired and burned out lately, and I was thinking about how much I would love to learn to paint. What do you think?" versus "You always get to do what you want and never let me have a moment to myself." These are extreme examples, but one encourages partnership, while the other sparks defensiveness.

Actively listen

Really try to hear the heart behind your partner's statements and don't just listen to respond. It can take effort to set aside your personal agenda, but after taking time to think about what your spouse's needs or wants might be, this will be easier to do. When your partner says something, be curious, paraphrasing what you hear (even if you don't agree). And ask for clarification by saying something like, "That's interesting. Tell me more." Aim to truly understand how your partner feels. Creating an empathetic atmosphere will encourage understanding in the relationship.

It's about give-and-take

You want something, but be willing to give a little, too. Relationships aren't about demands. They're about mutual understanding, compassion, and sacrifice. While you have thoughts on what you need, be open to what your spouse verbalizes, too. And I'd encourage you to take it one step further. Preemptively take some time to think through what your partner might be needing or wanting, and incorporate these thoughts into the conversation. Demonstrate that you have been considering them. Empathy goes a long way in deepening connection.

Do regular relationship checkups

It is so much easier to talk about things in a casual way when resentment, frustration, or utter exhaustion hasn't developed. Doing regular check-ins (like our nightly post-bedtime hangouts by the pond) provides a natural time and space to ask how the other is doing and to share ways that could help us flourish more. We have gotten in the habit of doing a weekly date day on a Saturday or

Sunday to go on a hike together or explore a new part of our city. You can take a walk around the neighborhood, have a special meal together after the kids are in bed, or even conduct a regular "board meeting" for your relationship and family. These conversations certainly don't need to take place every week, but having regular times mapped out is a helpful way to foster connection and open communication.

The day-in, day-out of raising children and fostering a thriving career can feel like that "lather, rinse, and repeat" cycle. But with some self-reflection, empathy for your partner, and thoughtful conversations, it can turn into "lather, *sing a bit in the shower,* rinse, repeat."

Adapted from content posted on hbr.org, April 22, 2020 (product #H05J42).

Too Much to Do? Here's How to Ask for Help

by Heidi Grant

Quick Takes

- Admit that you need to ask for help more
- Figure out exactly what you need
- Ask directly and clearly
- Accept the help that you are offered
- Say thank you

Raise your hand if you have an insurmountable pile of projects on your to-do list and an inbox so terrifying that you can hardly bear to behold it.

Cue the sea of arms waving wildly.

You have too much to do. You can't do it alone. You need people to help you. *Why aren't they helping you?!?*

Here's the uncomfortable truth: If you aren't getting the support you need with your crushing workload, odds are it's kind of your fault.

Cue the sea of angry readers arguing back right now.

What I mean is, you probably aren't asking for the support you actually need, and if you *are*, you probably aren't asking for it in the right way. Loads of studies have found that people have an innate desire to be helpful, by and large. (This is one reason the "givers" among us tend to get overwhelmed.) But even though people are much more likely to lend us a hand than we assume, most of us can't stand the idea of asking for help.

If you're drowning in work or other tasks right now, you need to get over that. Try the following steps.

Figure Out What You Actually Need

First, set aside time to figure out what, specifically, would *really* help you.

People who are drowning aren't always at their most rational and strategic. We may neglect to ask for help because we can't even make sense of what to ask *for*. And the last thing we want to do is stop and think about it—better to push ahead, alone and stressed to the point of breaking.

Just as it's said you have to spend money to make money, the truth is you sometimes have to spend a little time in order to save a lot of it. So, take a moment to go through everything on your plate. Identify tasks that someone could help you with that meet both of the following criteria:

- Having someone do it for you would provide significant relief or make you substantially more effective.

- Someone could do it for you without needing tons of supervision or explaining.

Ask for It Very Clearly

One of the most underestimated obstacles to *giving* help is uncertainty. No one wants to offer unwanted help—

people tend to get cranky when you do. If someone is unsure about whether you want help, how to help, or whether they can give you what you need, they aren't going to help you.

It's common for people who need to ask for help to be vague in how they ask for it, out of an aversion to the whole situation. Social psychologists have found, over and over, that asking for help fills us with intense discomfort—even, sometimes, a physical revulsion. So we couch our request for help as a question ("Would you like to . . . ?") or a favor ("If you have time . . ."). This leads to uncertainty, which leads to inertia.

It's up to *you* to take all that uncertainty away by:

- Making an explicit request for help

- Being very, very specific about what it is you want them to do, and when

- Being careful to choose someone who actually *can* help in the way you are asking

Accept Whatever Help You Are Offered

There are two ways in which we all tend to be overly rigid when it comes to accepting help, both of which can be self-defeating.

The first is being rigid about *the type of help* we are looking for. For example, I was doing research on a book and asked an acquaintance for assistance. He replied that he couldn't spare the time himself, but he offered a different type of help: an introduction to a few colleagues who might be able to help with it instead. I ultimately got exactly what I needed from one of those colleagues. The introduction, even though it wasn't what I asked for, was very helpful.

The second has to do with *whom we ask* for help. We all have a tendency to write off the people who have turned down our requests for help in the past. But the research on this one is very clear: People who have rejected your request for help in the past are actually more likely to help you the second time you ask.[1] This comes, more often than not, from a desire to repair the relationship that might have been damaged by the rejection—and, frankly, from not wanting to look like the kind of jerk who turns someone down twice. So don't hesitate to reach out to the people who have left you high and dry in the past—they may welcome a shot at redemption.

It's important to respect the fact that you haven't cornered the market on being overwhelmed—other people may be swamped too. This is not a reason *not* to ask; it's a reason to be flexible about the help you are offered, and from whom.

Say Thank You

Really, this last step should go without saying, but you can't take anything for granted these days. One of the most important motivators for helpers is the potential to feel effective. Studies show that when people can vividly imagine the impact their help will have—or, even better, can learn about the *actual* impact it had—they are more motivated to continue helping in the future.[2] Everyone wants to see their help land. It's up to you to make sure they do.

While these steps sound easy, I know they're not—if they were, you wouldn't be drowning in the first place. But remember, when it comes to getting the help you need, you have far better chances for success than you realize—if you'll only ask for it.

Adapted from "Drowning in Work? Here's How to Ask a Colleague for Help," on hbr.org, June 14, 2018 (product #H04ECF).

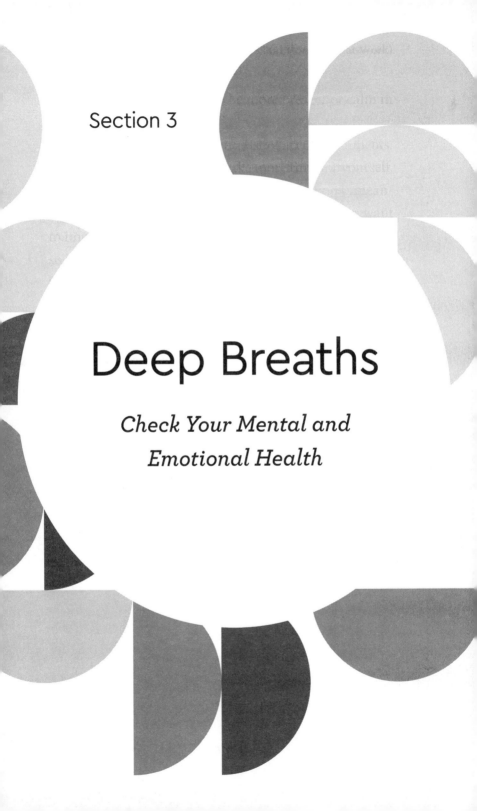

Section 3

Deep Breaths

*Check Your Mental and
Emotional Health*

Stop Feeling Guilty About What You Can't Get Done

by Art Markman

Quick Takes

- Allow yourself to let go of guilt and shame
- Forgive yourself for what you missed or couldn't finish
- Applaud yourself for the things you *have* accomplished
- Practice acceptance of your current situation

M ost people I know have a to-do list so long that it's not clear there's an end to it. Whether it's a list of projects for work or a pile of commitments at home, it's hard to find the time do it all. Some tasks, even quite important ones, linger unfinished for a long time, and it's easy to start feeling guilty or ashamed about what you have not yet completed—or what you're unable to do.

People experience guilt and its close cousin shame when they have done something wrong. Guilt is focused internally on the behavior someone has committed, while shame tends to involve feeling as if you are a bad person, particularly in the context of bad behaviors that have become public knowledge.

The fundamental question is whether these feelings are a good thing. To answer that, it's worth quoting from the movie *Bridge of Spies*. Mark Rylance plays the spy Rudolf Abel. He's asked at one point whether he is worried, and he responds, "Would it help?"

In this case, the answer is, "It depends."

Guilt can sometimes be motivating. For example, feelings of guilt can increase people's propensity to cooperate.[1] And, in some cases, guilt can also motivate people to make progress on projects that have stalled. At a minimum, guilt does not seem to make people worse at completing tasks. However, feeling guilty when you aren't in a position to do anything about it—for instance, when you're away from work—is not helpful and can be painful. It will make you feel worse about your job in general and spoil time that you could be spending with friends and family or engaging in an enjoyable activity.

Shame, though, is a different story. There is evidence that people will explicitly procrastinate to avoid shame.[2] Feeling shame about what you have not completed is likely to make the problem worse, not better, making it an emotion that is almost never helpful.

What can you do to avoid the negative effects of guilt and shame?

Exercise self-compassion

Being kind to and willing to forgive yourself has been shown to alleviate the negative effects of shame. Imagine that you are giving advice to someone else who is in the situation that you are in—to a friend who is behind on several projects, say, or a fellow parent who missed a volunteering event at school. Chances are that you'd be willing to tell other people to give themselves a break. You should be willing to give yourself the same advice.

Focus on your accomplishments

Psychologist Gabriele Oettingen's research demonstrates that focusing on the gap between what you *have* accomplished and what you *want to* accomplish leads to feelings of dissatisfaction. That energy can be motivating to act, but when you're not able to act, focusing on your accomplishments instead gives you a sense of pride in what you have done. Banish the guilt by feeling good about what you have already done, like how you finished your son's costume for the school play, were able to attend your daughter's speech for the Student Council, and successfully pitched a new client. When you are in a position to take action—say, sitting back at your desk on Monday morning—then you can make better use of the dissatisfaction that comes from focusing on what's not yet done.

Practice acceptance

One of the outcomes of many mindfulness techniques is an acceptance of your current situation.[3] This is also useful when you are trying to overcome feelings of guilt. In those moments, you need to remember that all of the work you have to do will be there when you get back to it, whether you feel guilty about it in the moment or not. In other words, remind yourself that feeling guilt at that moment doesn't help.

You want to use guilt as a motivational tool when you are in a position to get things done. When you're not, develop strategies to leave it behind. And find ways to reduce feelings of shame. Recognize that failing to get some work completed does not make you a bad person. It just makes you a person.

Adapted from "You're Never Going to Be 'Caught Up' at Work. Stop Feeling Guilty About It," on hbr.org, July 19, 2018 (product #H04FNR).

How to Refuel When You're Feeling Emotionally Drained

by Monique Valcour

Quick Takes

- Be aware of your emotional exhaustion and burnout
- Limit your exposure to circumstances that deplete you
- Conserve emotional resources using regulation techniques
- Connect with others, detach from work, and practice mindfulness

Emotional exhaustion lies at the heart of burnout. As your emotional resources are used up in trying to cope with challenging situations—such as overwhelming demands, conflict, or lack of support at work or at home—your sense of well-being and capacity to care for yourself and others are diminished.

In fact, research shows that people suffering from emotional exhaustion experience higher levels of work-life conflict.[1] They may find that they have less patience to engage with family and friends at the end of the day and become frustrated with them more easily. This can lead to feelings of guilt and loss.

Take my coaching client, Evelyn. A product manager in a medical device firm that's recently been acquired, she was struggling with a high level of uncertainty at work. Since the acquisition, she hasn't been getting reliable information from senior leadership and doesn't know whom to trust. Consequently, she can't provide clarity to her worried team, which makes her feel like an unreliable leader. She is disappointed at her boss's failure to advocate for the division and to demand greater clarity from the executives of the acquiring company. What's worse, the very qualities of the business that gave Evelyn a sense of purpose are being extinguished, leading her to question how long she can continue working there. The unsettling prospect of having to leave a job she once loved to protect her happiness is heightened by her status as the primary earner in her family and the contracting job market. The weight of these circumstances has left Evelyn emotionally exhausted.

Evelyn's husband, Jack, is a writer who's been working from home since before their 3-year-old son, Ben, and 7-year-old daughter, Judith, were born. Jack took care of the children while Evelyn worked. With the additional stress and her need to work remotely during the recent Covid pandemic, the boundaries between her personal and professional lives have collapsed, and Evelyn worries that she's performing poorly in both areas. She's annoyed when her children interrupt her calls when she's working from home and disappointed with herself for feeling that way. At the same time, her mind churns with anxiety about her job. She feels unable to shake her growing sense of dread and feels like a less joyful person than she used to be. On her worst days, she barely recognizes herself.

Evelyn's situation is not unique. Many of my coaching clients are also emotionally drained by aspects of their jobs, from an overwhelming workload to interpersonal conflict, from having to compromise their values to being ostracized, mistreated, or harassed.

Pushing back against emotional exhaustion requires a combination of three approaches: reducing the drain on your emotional resources, learning to conserve them, and regularly replenishing them. Imagine that you have an internal fuel tank and a gauge on your dashboard that lets you know how full it is. Some conditions cause your fuel to burn up quickly, just as extreme weather, rough terrain, carrying a heavy load, or accelerating and braking rapidly would use gas at a greater rate than normal on-the-road scenarios. To make sure you don't run low on fuel, you want to reduce your exposure to difficult conditions, drive more efficiently, and make sure you refuel regularly.

Reducing the Drain

The first step in reducing emotional resource consumption is recognizing the circumstances (for example, situations, tasks, relationships) that deplete you, then limiting your exposure to them.

Turning back to the case of Evelyn, there is not much she can do to change or avoid the shifting cultural dynamics at work in the wake of the acquisition. But she has realized that engaging in doomsday conversations with a particularly negative colleague heightens her anxiety, so Evelyn is no longer indulging in these exchanges. When her coworker starts complaining, Evelyn reminds her that, while they're not happy about the direction the company appears to be moving in, they'll both feel and perform better if they focus on what they can control, such as how they show up and relate to other people. Then she engages her counterpart in a conversation about what's going well.

Evelyn has also asked her boss to share any information he receives from senior leadership, even if it's incomplete. She has made it clear that she is better able to manage her team when she has a clearer view into what's happening at the top of the organization.

Learning to Conserve

The next step is learning to operate with greater emotional efficiency with emotion regulation techniques, such as recognizing and acknowledging your feelings and reappraising stressful experiences.

Evelyn uses two strategies to reframe what she experiences and how she thinks about it to conserve her emotional resources. The first is stepping outside of her own perspective and considering the larger context of her situation. She reminds herself that some of the disruption she's facing, although unpleasant, is normal in the context of mergers and acquisitions, and that those related to the pandemic have become a universal experience. When she remembers that she is one of many people going through such turmoil, it feels less personal.

The second strategy is staying connected to her core values and using them to navigate difficult situations.

Be Grateful More Often

by Francesca Gino

Feeling grateful has several beneficial effects on us: Gratitude enables us to savor positive experiences, cope with stressful circumstances, be resilient in the face of challenges, and strengthen our social relationships. Psychological research has shown that writing letters of gratitude once a week over a six-week period leads to greater life satisfaction as compared to simply recording ordinary life events.[a]

Counting our blessings doesn't just cheer us up; it can also improve our health and well-being. In a series of well-known studies, psychologists Robert Emmons and Michael McCollough asked participants to keep weekly journals for 10 weeks.[b] Some were asked to write about five things or people they were grateful for each week, some were asked to write about five hassles that they experienced during the week, and a third group was asked to write about any five events that occurred during the week. Participants asked to list hassles included the following: hard-to-find parking, spending their money too quickly, and burned macaroni and cheese. Those who listed blessings mentioned experiences such as the generosity of their friends, learning something interesting, and seeing the sunset through the clouds. Those in this gratitude group scored higher on measures of positive emotions, self-reported symptoms of their physical and mental health, and also felt more connected to others as compared to those who made routine notes about their days or wrote about hassles.

NOTES

a. Sonja Lyubomirsky, Kennon M. Sheldon, and David Schkade, "Pursuing Happiness: The Architecture of Sustainable Change," *Review of General Psychology* 9, no. 2 (2005): 111–131.

b. Robert A. Emmons and Michael E. McCullough, "Counting Blessing Versus Burdens: An Experimental Investigation of Gratitude and Subjective Well-Being in Daily Life," *Journal of Personality and Social Psychology* 84, 2 (2003): 377–389.

Adapted from content posted on hbr.org, November 26, 2013 (product #H00IL8).

Evelyn cares deeply about being honest and reliable. In coaching, we helped her find tangible anchors for these values by reflecting on what comes to mind when she thinks about the words *honesty* and *reliability.* She settled on an antique clock on her shelf—a gift from her beloved father—that still keeps perfect time. For her, it represents honesty and reliability. Whenever she looks at the clock, she renews her connection to these values and feels more capable of showing up as a positive and supportive leader her team can rely on.

Replenishing Your Fuel

The last critical strategy for preventing emotional exhaustion is making sure that you refuel. To overcome her fears about potentially having to find a new job, Evelyn is reaching out and renewing connections with people in her network. Through these conversations, she feels a stronger sense of belonging to her professional community, gathers valuable information about options available to her, and feels validated as a person who has much to offer. As a result, she feels much more hopeful. While she's not actively looking for another job at this time, she'll be better positioned if she does decide to.

Another way to boost reserves is to engage in non-work activities—like going for walks, connecting with friends over video chat, or pursuing hobbies like cooking or gardening. Doing so promotes relaxation, psychological detachment from work, and feelings of control and mastery. One insidious effect of emotional exhaustion is, when you're suffering from it, you may feel too tired to marshal the effort needed for exercise, social interaction, or hobbies. But you must.

Evelyn and her family came up with a creative ritual for joyfully reconnecting with one another. At six o'clock every evening, Jack puts on dance music and everyone dances together in the living room for 15 minutes. The kids look forward to it, the adults let go of the day's stresses, and they all laugh, smile, and enjoy being silly together.

Mindfulness practices, such as paying attention to your experiences from moment to moment, focusing on your breathing, spending 10 minutes thinking about what you're grateful for, or intentionally looking for what's positive, are yet another way to refuel. Research shows that people who do this at work experience lower levels of emotional exhaustion.[2]

Adopting the above practices doesn't mean you won't experience moments of stress and anxiety. But they will increase your resilience and resistance to emotional exhaustion.

Adapted from content posted on hbr.org, April 30, 2020 (product #H05I7Z).

12

Let Go of Perfectionism

by Alice Boyes

Quick Takes

- Distract yourself when you are ruminating on mistakes
- Imagine the critical voice in your head as a comical character
- Try restorative yoga and other relaxing practices
- Realize how parenting makes you better at your job and vice versa
- Cultivate relationships that encourage self-acceptance
- Acknowledge that culture is the cause for most judgment

When you're juggling work and parenting, it's inevitable that you'll drop a ball periodically. You'll chase someone down for information they already gave you. You'll lose your child's sun hat at the playground (if you remember to bring it at all). Your child will ask you to make banana cupcakes for three months before you finally get around to it. Or you'll read an email you need to reply to but promptly forget—and only remember when you're awake at 3 a.m.

While these slipups happen for everyone, for perfectionists, these instances feel like an emotional bee sting. Mistakes provoke anxiety for perfectionists and shake their sense of identity. Memories of past mistakes can pop back into mind long after the fact, and this can leave the person feeling as if they're doing a terrible job in all their roles—at home and work.

There are legitimate reasons working parents strive for perfection. When it comes to raising kids, the stakes feel very high, and perfection is culturally expected of parents. In the workplace, parents often feel pressure to demonstrate that they're just as career driven as they were before they had kids. Those who've used perfectionism as a strategy for high performance and to feel in control can start to feel as if their standards are impossible to maintain once they become parents, and this can cause tremendous anxiety.

While it's commendable to want to excel to the highest extent possible (and show your boss and coworkers that you can), obsessing over mistakes can do more harm than good.

Mistakes have two types of consequences. First, there are the *actual* consequences. In reality, many mistakes have no consequences at all. For instance, you put your child in their car seat and forget to buckle them in. When you arrive home, you're horrified to find the buckle unfastened. While this is certainly not a mistake you should repeat, ultimately you got home safely, and there were no immediate repercussions. The same might go for missing a deadline by a day or calling a fellow parent by the wrong name. When a mistake does have an objective consequence, it's more likely to be mild or moderate, as when you put off booking a flight and the price goes up. Major repercussions to common mistakes are few and far between.

The second type of consequences are the *psychological* consequences of mistakes. For perfectionists, nothing is a "small" mistake, because the objective consequences pale in comparison to the psychological fallout. When you're a perfectionist, mistakes trigger harsh self-criticism and intrusive overthinking. Anxious perfectionists in particular are often prone to catastrophizing mistakes, like imagining "what if I'd had an accident on the way home" and envisioning their child dying after not being fastened in. Or, an anxious perfectionist who messes up one deadline might start to panic that it's the start of a pattern, even if it only happens rarely. Or they begin to question their identity as a conscientious, well-regulated person. In other scenarios, mistakes can be irritating, like wearing a scratchy fabric. For instance, you intended to use some rewards before they expired, and you forgot, and you're annoyed with yourself. This type of irritation sucks up mental bandwidth and drains you.

This difficulty in psychologically tolerating mistakes can get in the way of improvement. If you start loading up on self-criticism, you're likely to turn your guilt ("I screwed up") into shame ("I am a screw-up"). There's an abundance of research showing that self-compassion—rather than self-criticism—after mistakes or poor performance makes it more likely people will take objective steps to improve.

Part of the issue is in rumination. Replaying your mistake and the decisions leading up to it often feels like problem solving. But this rehashing actually makes it less likely you will take objective steps to do better. Rumination can also be distracting, leading you to engage in more behaviors you regret, like ignoring your child's attempts to get your attention because you're thinking about what went wrong at work.

Fortunately, there are ways that working parents can overcome their perfectionist tendencies, learn more self-compassion, and snap themselves out of rumination. Here are some specific strategies for how to tolerate imperfections.

Disrupt rumination with absorbing distractions

I experienced a failed IVF cycle recently. After getting the news I wasn't pregnant, I spent five hours building a robot kit with my 4-year-old. It was the perfect fiddly, novel activity to take my mind off of replaying everything I might've done differently. Doing projects (crafts, baking, STEM experiments) or playing games with your children is an excellent strategy for disrupting rumination. People think cognitive-absorbing distraction is too simple a strategy to work when they're very distressed, but it does. If you prefer to take time for yourself, try puzzles, challenging games, or any type of hands-on tinkering.

Externalize the perfectionist voice in your head

Give your perfectionist self-talk a quirky character and exaggerate the way it speaks to you. For instance, you might imagine a grubby, little potato-chip-eating gremlin who bosses you around and points out everything in your house that hasn't been picked up. This technique works by helping you get psychological distance from your perfectionist thoughts. Humor can also help you treat the thoughts more lightly. By exaggerating, you make the thoughts more absurd, which can help you recognize your absurd standards.

Try restorative yoga

I absolutely hit the wall recently, but I didn't think I'd done enough work that I should be tapped out. In reality, I'm still dealing with grief about my failed IVF cycle; I'm doing another cycle, which means I'm on medications that are messing with my emotions; and I'm feeling anxious about how it will go and how much it's costing. To help, I did a 20-minute restorative yoga routine, and the next day I bounced back and had better-than-average productivity. Restorative yoga is basically directed lying down with various supports that allow you to fully relax—it doesn't remotely resemble exercise. Restorative and yin yoga tend to feel very self-compassionate. Open awareness meditation can also help with rumination. You can easily Google or search YouTube for do-it-yourself resources once you know the terms to search. If what you find is too New Agey for you, adapt it so you're more comfortable. Using these types of practices, even just occasionally, can help on days you feel as if nothing you do is good enough.

Recognize how parenting makes you better at your job—and vice versa

Another strategy to prevent feeling pulled in two directions is to list the ways that being a parent makes you better at your core work role, and vice versa. Your responses will be specific to your life, but for me, I've been more focused on meaningful work since I've had a kid. Small blips at work feel less existentially threatening, since they pale in comparison to whether my kid is healthy and happy. And parenting has given me greater confidence in my capabilities, which has translated into greater confidence in my work. On the flip side, all the emotion regulation skills I've learned through my work have made me better able to manage my own and my child's emotions. Looking at your time at work and home in this way can change your perspective and give you more freedom to make mistakes or let go.

Cultivate work relationships that support your self-acceptance

Over time (years not months), build up work relationships with people who help you feel more self-accepting. Develop relationships with people whom you trust and respect enough that you don't mind getting corrective feedback from that person. Cultivate collegial relationships that feel more "iron sharpens iron" than directly

A Different View on "Doing It All"

Many working parents struggle with the guilt in doing things the "right" way or how they "should" be parenting. Every child is different, and so is every family. Looking at how you parent from a different perspective can alleviate the guilt when you feel you're falling short.

Consider this story from Caitlyn Collins, author of *Making Motherhood Work: How Women Manage Careers and Caregiving*, that she shared in an interview on the *HBR IdeaCast*:

> I had a single, working mom for much of my childhood who did it all—or at least she strived to do it all. She had a very successful career in corporate sales and marketing. And that often meant sacrificing time at home.
>
> So, we had an absolute army of caregivers—babysitters, nannies, sports teams, clubs, neighbors— taking care of us until she could get home at the end of the day. She typically worked seven to seven in the office.

competitive. These relationships will help you feel more emotionally stable. Plus, we know that teams and management relationships in which people can take creative risks without worrying about interpersonal rejection or diminished social standing perform better.

I remember really being in awe of my mom growing up. Seeing her leave in these impeccably tailored
suits and high heels, commanding these rooms full of
men in suits, but she was stressed and frantic. And
she tells me today that she constantly felt guilty and
inadequate.

We ate a lot of pizza and McDonald's, and she's
told me that she felt acutely guilty for having served
us those meals. I laughed when she admitted that
to me as an adult because I remember thinking that
I had the best mom ever because I got McDonald's
and pizza all the time. I thought she was just reward-
ing us. She told me, no, it's because I didn't have time
to get to the grocery store.

And I said, well, I just thought that made you an
extra cool mom.

Adapted from "Why U.S. Working Moms Are So Stressed—and What
to Do About It," on *HBR IdeaCast* (podcast), March 26, 2019.

Acknowledge the systemic issues at play

Especially for working moms, there are pitfalls to not
being perfect. Women's mistakes get judged more harshly
and are remembered longer than men's, productivity

strategies like writing shorter emails can backfire for women, and people who choose flexible work options can be judged negatively. Choosing when and when not to be a perfectionist is a complex issue. If you acknowledge these factors and see these subtleties, you can make better case-by-case decisions about when to aim for perfection and when you can let some things slide. When you have strategies in your toolkit, like the ones I've outlined here, you can more adeptly turn your perfectionism on and off.

Working parents can feel many internal and external pressures to be perfect, but realistically it's impossible, and having such a mindset can rob you of enjoyment both at home and at work. Letting go of perfectionism is part science and part art, requiring knowledge of scientifically supported strategies (like those for disrupting rumination and increasing self-compassion) and personal experimentation to see which strategies work best for you. By understanding why you fall prey to perfectionistic tendencies and discovering how you can benefit by letting them go, you can find a way to have less stress and feel more present and productive at home and work.

Adapted from "How Working Parents Can Let Go of Perfectionism," on hbr.org, April 6, 2020 (product #H05HXF).

How Busy Working Parents Can Make Time for Mindfulness

by Michelle Gale

Quick Takes

- Note what you do each day and see where mindfulness can fit

- Practice meditation on your commute

- Pause throughout your workday to notice your body and breath

- Take a moment to be grateful at the dinner table

- Do a head-heart-gut check-in at bedtime

I t seems everywhere you look these days someone is touting the benefits of mindfulness—a practice that Jon Kabat-Zinn, the founder of Mindfulness-Based Stress Reduction, describes simply as "paying attention in a particular way: on purpose, in the present moment, and non-judgmentally." Research shows that people who practice mindfulness are less stressed, more focused, and better able to regulate their emotions.[1]

But, if you're a busy working parent, how do you build mindfulness into an already packed day? Those of us with kids and jobs often feel tired and rushed. We're constantly multitasking, juggling personal and professional responsibilities, and feeling stressed about all we can't get done. According to a Pew Research Center analysis, 56% of working parents say they find it difficult to balance their time between work and family.[2] Though I now counsel others on how to break this cycle, I can certainly relate to it.

Years ago, I worked as Twitter's head of learning and development when the company was growing 350% year after year. It was like being on a rocket ship, and I loved the work. But I found myself struggling to stay connected to my family. I can remember the afternoon my son's school called to make me aware that no one had come to pick him up. He was in first grade at the time, and I burst into tears.

Although I was already committed to a mindfulness practice (I would sometimes sneak away to the meditation and yoga room we had in the office), I was still having trouble figuring out a way to weave presence and awareness into my day. Here's the solution that I came up with and now recommend to others.

Start by spending a few minutes writing down what you do each day. It might look something like this: wake up, coffee, family breakfast, pack lunches, prep for school day, walk dog, shower for work, drive car, train ride, walk to office, work all day, walk to train, car ride home, dinner, bath time, family reading or games, bedtime. Even if you work from home and have no commute, you can likely come up with a similar list of things you do each day.

Now consider where mindfulness practice can fit in. For example:

Coffee: Pause before the first sip. Smell the aroma, feel the heat of the mug on your hand, and take three intentional breaths. Now enjoy.

Train ride: Once you're settled into your seat, set a timer for 5 to 10 minutes and practice meditation. Sit in silence and focus on your breathing or use a mindfulness app on your phone to listen to a guided meditation. Your eyes can be open or closed depending on the situation and what feels safe or comfortable.

Work: Each time you sit down to your computer, take a pause. Close your eyes, notice the sensation of your feet on the floor, your body in your chair, feel your breath come in and out of your body. Continue with your day.

Dinner: As you are preparing the meal, spend a moment reflecting on where the food came from. Imagine who planted it, picked it, or delivered it to the store where you purchased it. On occasions when your entire family is sitting around the table at the same time, take a moment to feel grateful.

Bedtime: Decide on a ritual that cultivates mindful awareness. For younger children, consider having them put a stuffed animal on their belly as each of you count how many times the animal rides up and down with their breath. If your children are older, try a head-heart-gut check-in at bedtime. Is the mind busy or calm in this moment? Are any emotions present or lingering from the day? Is there anything that needs to be shared or said that has not been already?

Does mindfulness seem a little more doable now? Research indicates that it takes just eight weeks of relatively regular practice to make positive changes to the brain.[3] But if we wait until we have enough bandwidth to devote big blocks of time to it, we may never start. For working parents, my advice is to instead insert just a few small moments of mindfulness into your day, even—and especially—when life seems too busy, hectic, and out of control.

Adapted from content posted on hbr.org, November 22, 2017 (product #H040MH).

Section 4

Time for Your Checkup

Prioritize Physical Well-Being

How Regular Exercise Helps You Balance Work and Family

by Russell Clayton

Quick Takes

- Exercise regularly to reduce stress and be more productive

- Use physical activity to increase your self-efficacy

- Reserve time before or after work to go for a bike ride or swim laps

- Take short breaks in your workday for a walk, run, or workout

I f you have been feeling torn between exercising more and being a better working parent or spouse, then this should come as great news: You can do both. Carving out regular time in your schedule for physical activity can mean success, happiness, and less stress in your future.

Consider this example: Matthew Beason is a well-respected executive at a nonprofit with a multibillion-dollar endowment. On top of continual domestic travel, countless dinners with donors, and constant planning meetings, Matthew is also a married father of four. While his work schedule sometimes leaves him exhausted, Matthew consistently attends school and athletic events and is, while at home, fully there for his family.

Likewise, Luke McKelvy, owner of McKelvy Wealth Management, has a busy schedule of meeting with current and prospective clients and setting up his new business. Luke is the father of two children, twin boys under the age of two. Like Matthew, he manages to square the priority he places on his family's happiness with the demands of work he considers important.

Matthew and Luke have pulled off the neat trick of successfully integrating work and life mainly through a skillful alignment of their priorities. But something else about them, it turns out, has probably helped: their adherence to regular exercise. Research by my colleagues and I demonstrates a clear relationship between physical activity that is planned, structured, repetitive, and purposive—to use Carl J. Caspersen and colleagues' seminal definition of exercise—and one's ability to manage the intersection between work and home.[1]

My colleagues and I surveyed a population of working adults to gather input regarding both their exercise habits and their experience of resolving work and home demands. Briefly, those respondents who reported regular exercise were less likely to experience conflict between their work and home roles.

That's a somewhat counterintuitive finding. An exercise regimen, after all, draws on scarce time—and often disappears from professionals' lives for exactly that reason. How could adding it to an already busy schedule help resolve work-home trade-offs?

The pathways became evident in our research. First, and least surprisingly, exercise reduces stress, and lower stress makes the time spent in either realm more productive and enjoyable. In Luke's words, "Exercise allows me to leave my cares behind and provides me with time to think." A reduction in stress is tantamount to an expansion of time.

Second, we found that exercise helps work-home integration via increased *self-efficacy*. The term refers to the sense that one is capable of taking things on and getting them done—and although self-efficacy is a matter of self-perception, it has real impact on reality. According to psychologist Albert Bandura, who first proposed the concept, people with high self-efficacy are less likely to avoid difficult tasks or situations, and more likely to see them as challenges to be mastered. Our research suggests that people who exercise regularly enjoy greater self-efficacy, and it carries over into their work and home roles. The theory resonates with Matthew. As he puts it, "An hour of exercise creates a feeling that lasts well beyond that hour spent at the gym." Or take it from Luke, who competes in triathlons: "When I accomplish something during an exercise training session, I feel more confident in my professional and personal life."

So, see this as another reason to stick to that New Year's resolution to exercise. Or if that wasn't already your intention, consider what form of regular exercise would work best for you. Some people make it their habit to exercise prior to starting the workday because it's so easy to find reasons *not* to exercise later in the day. (I am personally fond of high-intensity interval training [HIIT], in part because of its short-duration workouts. I combine a few HIIT sessions with a couple of runs per week.) Others benefit from a break in the workday, especially when they can take advantage of on-site workout facilities or walk their dog around the neighborhood. Matthew's exercise routine entails heading out on his lunch break to run up and down the steps at a local football stadium. According to him, breaking up the workday with exercise "makes my problems get smaller" in the afternoon. Still others like the "wind-down time" of exercising after work. Luke tends to go for a bike ride or swim laps in the pool of his local fitness center after leaving the office. Whatever time and setting you prefer—taking long walks, joining a dance or Pilates class—the key is to engage in a level of exercise that dissipates stress and adds to your sense of what you are capable of.

Managers and HR professionals should take note, as well. It's important to organizational performance that people find ways to successfully integrate work and home demands. This research suggests that companies will benefit from removing constraints on employee exercise. By embracing more flexible working hours, for example, workplaces and supervisors can make it easier for people to find time for physical activity. More proactively, employers can encourage new habits like walking meetings or using the stairs as StairMasters. They might even offer "booster breaks" for employees to spend 10–15 minutes participating in stretching, breathing, and light aerobic routines.

Perhaps more than anything, employers can help by getting the word out that exercise isn't a selfish indulgence that inevitably requires some sacrifice on either the work or home front. What we found was overwhelming support for a positive relationship between regular exercise and satisfying management of the work-home interface. It isn't only that exercise supports better physical health. Through its direct impact on increased self-efficacy and reduced psychological strain, exercise leads to better integration of professional and personal lives.

Adapted from content posted on hbr.org, January 3, 2014 (product #H00M30).

Find Exercise in Life's Margins

by Nick Crocker

Quick Takes

- Aim for progress, not perfection
- Let go of setbacks and self-judgment
- Set weeklong goals, not longer
- Find something you enjoy doing
- Make small changes to daily habits

You consider yourself a fit, active person. But, like most busy professionals, you want to exercise more. You want to hit the gym more frequently; you want to finally start taking that yoga class or make that 7 a.m. boot camp in the local park. And then time and again, life just gets in the way. You're too busy. You work too late. The kids are sick. You book a breakfast meeting. You have work and social commitments that you just can't miss. And in all the chaos, exercise gets squeezed out. This, in reality, is most people's experience of exercise.

The reality is that those spare hours in the week are not going to materialize. We need to come up with a different solution. The key is to find exercise in the daily flow of your life. Doing so will boost your productivity, performance, and job satisfaction.

First, reset your expectations

Exercise has no lower limit. Every bit counts. But setting the bar too high is a recipe for consistent failure. Your exercise goal this week should be your current average minutes of exercise per week plus five. Next week's goal should be to add five more. The mistake many successful people make is to assume that it's all or nothing. Either you're training for a marathon or you're doing nothing at all. The goal in all cases should be progress, not perfection.

Have a short memory

They say great NFL quarterbacks need to have short memories. If they make a mistake, they forget it quickly and move on. The last bad pass shouldn't impact their shot at the next great one. The same goes for exercise. Forget sedentary days and weeks immediately. Your exercise past is not your exercise future. Deeming yourself an exercise failure is a relative and pointless judgment to make.

Plan to miss one week every month

When you're planning a new exercise routine, expect to lose one week out of four to a mixture of work travel, holidays, events (weddings, bar mitzvahs, Super Bowls), sickness, injury, and unexpected intervening events. If you expect life to go smoothly, you are in for a shock. There will always be disruptions. It's not about how you exercise in a good week; it's about how quickly you recover from a bad one.

Set seven-day goals

You can plan with reasonable certainty what you will be doing four days from now. Four weeks is much harder to divine. So, make all your exercise goals fit within a seven-day period. After seven days, set new goals for the following week. That way, you don't overwhelm yourself with change. It's compartmentalized and easier for the mind to process. And don't tie exercise to weight goals. If you attempt the two with too much intensity, you're likely to crash. Exercise is a constant, not an intervention to solve a problem.

Orient to social and playful

Over time, you'll orient toward pleasure and away from pain. If exercise is painful, you're doing it wrong. If you hate the rowing machine, then stop doing it. Find exercise that feels playful or enjoyable for you. Walking, gardening, climbing, hiking, kayaking. And if possible, make it social, too. Our minds seek play and social connection naturally. If we couch exercise in those two concepts, we can transform the experience.

Exercise in the margins

Instead of taking the elevator at work, take the stairs. Once in the morning, once at night, and twice (up and down) when you go for lunch. Instead of getting off at your normal bus stop, get off one stop early and walk the rest of the way to work. Do the same on the way home. Once a week, take a walk while you call your mother (or any other deserving family member). If phone conversations aren't your thing, see if you can schedule one of your regular meetings as a walking meeting and talk business while you walk.

The reality is that most people can't exercise in the conventional "weights and treadmill at the gym" way more than once or twice a week. And many struggle with even that. This is a hard truth that will not change. Finding exercise in your day's margins is the only way to start living a sustainable, active life.

Adapted from content posted on hbr.org, May 23, 2012.

How Working Parents Can Prioritize Sleep

by Amie M. Gordon and Christopher M. Barnes

Quick Takes

- Set a consistent sleep routine—and stick to it
- Limit blue light and keep screens out of your bedroom
- Avoid talking about serious matters before bed
- Make the most of your family's sleeping schedules
- Shape your work schedule around your family
- Don't stress about a bad night's sleep

When you're juggling a job, kids, and all the details of everyday life, sleep feels like a luxury you can afford later, when your kids are grown. Instead of sleeping, parents use those precious few moments they have at the end of the day to catch up on work or take some much-needed "me time." But the problems that come with not getting enough sleep won't simply step aside and wait until retirement. Sleep deprivation magnifies the challenges in an already difficult life. One area where sleep deprivation takes its toll is on our relationships, both at home and in the workplace.

Research from across the globe has linked general sleep tendencies with relationship quality, showing that people who sleep worse experience less satisfying relationships, particularly with romantic partners. People are more likely to fight with their partners after a poor night of sleep, and couples have more difficulty resolving conflicts if *either* partner slept worse the prior night. The effects go the other way as well—people tend to sleep worse after fighting with their romantic partners.[1] This creates the possibility of a vicious cycle in which poor sleep begets conflict, and conflict begets poor sleep. Additionally, research suggests children who are exposed to more marital conflict tend to sleep worse, which may have further negative effects on the parents' sleep. In contrast, children whose parents have higher-quality relationships tend to sleep better.[2]

Sleep also plays a role in how we relate to our children. One study found that mothers who had more disrupted sleep were less sensitive to their 18-week-old infants than those who had more continuous sleep. Good sleep may also be a protective factor; both parents and children who sleep better are more resilient in the face of stressors.[3] Overall, getting the sleep we need helps us have better relationships with our children.

Although our sleep tends to happen at home, we bring the consequences of poor sleep into the workplace, too. Leaders who report sleeping worse tend to engage in more abusive behaviors toward their employees (such as yelling at them in front of their colleagues) and have damaged relationships with those employees. Sleep-deprived leaders are also less charismatic and generally less effective in their leadership roles. Research indicates that overall, businesses benefit when employees are well rested.[4]

Deprioritizing sleep is one way to deal with the heavy demands on a working parent's limited time, but the consequences are clear: Both at home and in the workplace, relationships are worse when people don't prioritize their sleep.

So, what is a time-famished working parent to do?

Set Habits for Better Sleep

Since physicists have yet to unlock the secrets to freezing time, working parents must turn to more feasible means to get a good night of sleep. Here are a few evidence-based tips to help working parents take care of themselves and create good sleeping practices when it seems like there is no time to do so. Getting good sleep won't give you more time, but it will help you make better use of the time you have.

Make sleep a priority

Recognize that your days will feel more productive if you get enough sleep, which can give you a sense of having more time. There's always the desire to fit in "one last thing" or put off going to sleep, but a good night of sleep will give you much-needed resources to deal with the demands of daily life. Figure out how much sleep you need to feel well rested (the recommendation in the United States is seven to nine hours for adults). Decide what time you need to wake up in the morning, then count backward. Set a bedtime alarm, giving yourself an extra 30 minutes to an hour to unwind and get ready for bed each night. Creating a relaxing bedtime routine for the whole family (dim lights, relaxing music, stories in bed) might be one way to get everyone to wind down together.

Set a consistent sleep routine for yourself and your children

One of the best ways to sleep well is to have a consistent sleep routine. This tells your body when to wake up and when to go to sleep so that it releases melatonin at the right time, making it easier to fall asleep and stay asleep. A consistent routine won't just get you more sleep, it will get you more high-quality sleep. Keep these habits both on the days you're working and on the days you're not. Although it is enticing, using the weekends to do a major "catch-up" on sleep is actually counterproductive. Sleeping in late will feel good that day, but it throws off your body clock and fails to address the larger issue of having a consistent schedule that allows enough time for sleep on a daily basis. Children, even teens, get more sleep when parents help structure the child's sleep schedule.

Limit exposure to blue light at night

Smartphones, computers, and tablets emit blue light, which tells your body it's daytime and can disrupt your sleep. To prevent this, use blue-light filters (built into most tablets and smartphones) or wear blue-light blocking glasses when using a screen in the hours leading up to your bedtime routine. On the other hand, exposure to bright blue light in the morning is a great way to start your day. Exposure to bright light when you first wake up helps set your circadian rhythm and lets your body know it's time to be alert.

Keep screens out of your bedroom

In an ever-connected world, working parents may want to check their email one last time or scroll through Twitter for a few minutes after they're in bed. But a big part of good sleep hygiene is giving your body a chance to unwind before you fall asleep. We also tend to lack self-regulation when we get more tired, so while you might only intend to go online for a few minutes, those handful of minutes can quickly turn into an hour or more. Leave your screens outside the room or put them in airplane mode before you get in bed.

Quit while you're ahead

We've all wanted to stay up just a little longer to finish the task we're working on. But if you're trying to work when it's time to go to bed, you're going to be more inefficient and make more mistakes. Instead, stick to your bedtime and return to your task the next day when you'll be refreshed, thinking clearly, and can get it done in half the time.

Don't stress about those inevitable nights of poor sleep

While a consistent sleep routine is great, everyone experiences poor sleep at some point. Worrying about your sleep can become a problem of its own. Instead, recognize that your body is resilient and can handle short-term sleep problems, and find ways to destress before bed to help you relax and sleep well.

Work with Those Around You

Beyond ways to make your sleep more consistent and habitual, consider these relationship-based strategies to prevent the inevitable conflicts that can arise from lack of sleep.

Don't talk about serious matters right before bed

Although you've likely been told to never go to bed angry, a good night of sleep might also help you deal more constructively with conflict. If you can, save serious matters for a time when you're both awake and have the energy to talk. This may seem impossible, but like sleep, building in time to talk when you aren't tired can help the rest of your relationship run more smoothly.

Everybody's Tired

The people in your life are likely just as tired as you are, so if your partner forgets to call you on their way home from work, assume it's because they had a difficult workday and not because they don't value your time. If your child is only giving one-word answers at dinner, remind yourself they may just be exhausted from an active day at school and not uninterested in what you have to say. And when your colleague forgets to confirm a meeting, check to see how they're doing personally before writing them off as unreliable.

Don't jump to conclusions or react unhappily. Give your family and colleagues the benefit of the doubt. Perhaps they could just use a good night's sleep.

Make the most of different sleeping schedules

Having a different bedtime from your partner might seem problematic when your schedules don't overlap—whether those differences are due to personal preferences or work schedules. However, you may be able to leverage this difference by putting the person who wakes up early in charge of the morning routine and the night owl in charge of bedtime.

Look into the possibility of flextime

If your job allows it, being able to work from home or shape your work schedule around your family might help you feel less stressed and sleep better. For example, if you're an early riser, you might benefit from working at home in the morning before your family gets up and adjusting your hours accordingly. Consider being flexible with your family time as well. For instance, some families with full schedules might find that breakfast together works better than the traditional family dinner, so you can devote those evening hours to attending your children's extracurricular activities, cementing a toddler's bedtime routine, or unwinding after a long day, without the added stress of meal prep.

When you feel as if you have no time to sleep is exactly when you need sleep the most. Finding a way to prioritize consistent, high-quality sleep can help you better navigate the demands of your everyday life, from better interactions with your family to better sleep for your children to better relationships at work.

Adapted from content posted on hbr.org, March 31, 2020 (product #H05HR7).

Parents, Take Your Sick Days

by Tim Sullivan

Quick Takes

- Commit to taking time off when you're not feeling well
- Try working from home—but only if you're well enough
- Be direct when you call in sick
- Create standard practices with your team for sick time
- Set expectations with your family for when parents are sick

Recently, I did something radical: I took a sick day. I hadn't been well for a few days, but I'd dutifully worked per usual. When I woke up on day three at 4:30 in the morning sicker than ever, I realized that I had to actually take time off. Like, really take time off—no email, no memo writing, no "just checking in." So, I did: I napped, played video games, cuddled the dog, watched Netflix, drank some broth. By the end of the day, I felt better.

And that meant that my sick day—atypical as it was—was better for me, my team at work, and my family.

This last group is especially pertinent to me. I've been a working father for over 20 years, and I've managed folks with kids at home for more than a decade. We've all heard the phrase "moms and dads don't get sick days," meaning that they're on the hook not only for themselves but for their kids too, and therefore unable to take time off. Ever. But the reality is that, despite their reluctance, working parents have to take care of themselves by taking time off when they need it.

That's a lesson that I've learned the hard way over time. I used to be reluctant to take my sick days. Before the Covid-19 pandemic, I can't tell you how many times I went to the office with a low-grade fever or a bad cough. I still have residual pangs of guilt when I use my sick days, even though I know better now. I'm not alone. According to a 2019 survey of 2,800 workers in the United States, 90% of employees said they often or always went to work when they were sick.[1] According to another survey from 2017, one in five full-time employees didn't take any sick time in the last year (a stat that gets worse for older workers), and almost 60% of workers took fewer than five days.[2]

There are a few reasons why we still work when sick. Employees report feeling as if they're burdening their colleagues with additional work. Some fret that the company will collapse without them. (It won't.) Others say that they feel as if their organization makes it difficult to take any time off at all. Plus, we fear the "mountain of work" we'll return to. Contingent or part-time workers may not get any sick days, let alone other paid time off, and working parents who use their sick time to take care of kids (an option in some, but not all states) can be understandably reluctant to use it on themselves.

Yet, there are good reasons for working parents to take the time they need to recuperate and take care of themselves:

- Taking the necessary time to recover will shorten your sickness, so you can get back on your feet faster.

- Your family is relying on you. Pushing through the week just to crash on Saturday means you may miss opportunities to go hiking, visit friends, or take part in some other favorite family activity.

- Taking time for yourself communicates your priorities and models behaviors to others—both at work and at home. If you want your kids to grow up to take care of themselves and work in a healthy environment, prioritizing your own health helps them see that it's OK.

- Finally, "being sick" doesn't mean that you're down with a fever, chills, stomach cramps, and odd rashes. Mental health days are just as important. Taking mental health seriously can have an outsized impact on family life by reenergizing you to engage with your partner and your kids.

So how do you actually go about taking the time you need? What are the things you need to consider in terms of logistics and schedules?

First, assess if you're well enough to work productively at home. Always talk with your manager, but sometimes canceling meetings and video calls, so you can email, work on spreadsheets, or cold-call in your pajamas for a day will get you where you need to be. That said, don't do this if your physical or mental state means you're going to do work that's subpar. If you do, you'll have to do it over again when you're feeling better. (As someone who has had to apologize for emails sent in the haze of the flu, trust me on this one.)

If you do call in sick, be direct. You don't have to be elaborate about your reason: "I'm not feeling well enough to work today, so I'm taking a sick day. I'll be back on the job tomorrow if I'm feeling better." Some organizations or managers may push back on this, but you don't owe them details about your health. If you've determined that you're not well enough to work, stay firm. Remember, this is your time and your health.

Also, work with your team to come up with a standard practice when it comes to being sick. My team and I decided that our standard is not to work when we're sick, period. That includes turning off email and group chats. It was hard to stick to the first time around (OK, I ruined it for everyone). But after renewing the pledge more recently, we've been able to stick to our plan, to everyone's benefit.

You may also want to communicate clearly with your partner about making sure you take care of each other by encouraging self-care. For instance, my wife and I let each other know when we would benefit from one of us taking a sick day—a concept that extends beyond simply not working and includes a break from childcare, errands, meal prep, and so on. And if we're both sick, we try to agree about who gets the first day, knowing that we will reverse roles next time.

Tell your kids about your routine, too, so they can learn early how to value their own health. Be straightforward: "You know that I would like to be able to work, but I'm not feeling well. It's important to take time to rest so that you can feel better." (Yes, these words will come back to haunt you when it's time for school, but that's OK.)

Finally, remember the larger picture. If this standard—serious self-care—becomes the bar for everyone, then we'll all be supporting one another, at home and at work. That's as it should be.

You won't be able to perform your best at work or at home if you're sick or not feeling well. Take the time you need to recuperate and care for yourself. You owe it to yourself—and those around you.

Section 5

Recess

Make Your Time Off Matter

The Case for Having Hobbies

by Scott Behson

Quick Takes

- Choose an activity that helps you hone new skills

- Spend time with family, including your kids

- Volunteer and contribute to your community

- Commit the time

A s a working parent, you're familiar with putting the needs of others before your own. You take care of your family first, and by working hard in your career, you often prioritize your clients', managers', and employer's time before carving out time for yourself.

But, as cliché as it may seem, airlines have it right when they advise you to put on your oxygen mask first before assisting others. After all, we're no good to anyone else if our energy is depleted. This is an especially difficult challenge as more of us work from home, eroding barriers between work and family time. But we can better take care of ourselves—and by extension, others—by spending some time tending to our own needs. A great way to do that is by taking on a hobby.

Many parents probably feel as if they don't have time for a hobby right now. But considered broadly, a hobby is simply the intentional, purposeful use of the time you do have for yourself (however short that window may be). Hobbies don't just take our mind off our stressors; they can help us meet our work and life challenges. Among other benefits, hobbies can help us achieve the following.

Relax and Recharge

My neighbor has a stressful job dealing with family-related mental health and trauma—the kind of work that could easily overwhelm. I most often see her in the evenings as she peacefully tends to her garden. She tells me that the consistent time she spends outside, doing the many simple things to help her vegetables grow, helps take her mind off her work. This improves her mood so she can be a more present parent and return to work more enthusiastically the next day.

Hone New Skills

Many hobbies involve study and practice of things we find enjoyable. If we pluck away at a guitar for an hour every other day, we can learn new songs, develop our skills, and get the intrinsic satisfaction of improving, even if no one else hears us play. The fact that we get better at something through hard work is intrinsically satisfying. We can also intentionally choose new hobbies to learn different skills, such as photography, brushing up on high-school Spanish, or starting a blog. Sometimes these new skills become things we can apply more broadly in our lives and jobs or can even start us on a new career.

Become Better Problem Solvers

Ever get stuck on a work problem, and then get the needed bolt of inspiration while folding the laundry? Solutions often come to us when we shift from focused thinking to diffuse thinking. Sometimes the best strategy is to take our mental focus off a problem—giving our brains an opportunity to subconsciously and creatively problem solve—all while we bake bread or build new bookshelves.

Connect with Others

We can use hobbies to spend valuable time with important people in our lives and to support those around us. If, like most working parents, you don't spend enough time with friends, you can use a hobby to create more social time. Why not get three of your friends to sign up for the same yoga class? Or, when you can't go to the studio, find a class you can all do over video. This way, you get regularly scheduled exercise and time with friends every week.

Hobbies can also provide more opportunities to spend time with family. If you and your spouse or partner feel as if you need more time together that doesn't involve chores or taking care of the kids, look for something you can do that you might both enjoy. Shared hobbies like reading the same book, going on nature walks, or figuring out how to roast, grind, and brew the perfect cup of coffee can be an investment in your relationship.

Many working parents also want the time they're spending with their kids to be more meaningful. Developing a common hobby with them is a great way to carve out quality time and to make memories. My family bakes together, but you can also consider art projects, a new LEGO set, or researching family history. Fun activities with you and your kids also provide unexpected opportunities for honest conversations, laying the groundwork for more adult relationships with them later on.

Finally, hobbies are a great way to meet others in your neighborhood and to contribute to your community, even virtually. Getting involved with a local charity or church group can help you develop skills, make friends, and give back to others. For example, my gardening neighbor met a lot of friends at our town's community garden, and she and her husband work with a community group to improve our local park. These days, many local schools and organizations are ramping up fundraising, food drives, and deliveries to the elderly and housebound. In many cases, you can even be involved online.

Keep in mind that you won't gain the benefits of hobbies unless you commit to them. Carve out regularly scheduled times for hobbies and protect that time as you would an important business meeting or family matter.

We are far more likely to follow through on a plan if we make it a set part of our schedule. Otherwise, it is easy to put off important activities because something more urgent pops up or because we're feeling lazy. You may love knitting, but a call from work might scuttle your plan. But if you joined a weekly knitting circle (even on a video platform like Zoom), you'll shut off your phone for that hour. If you enjoy playing basketball, don't just hope for a pick-up game every now and then; join a league at your local Y. Or sign up for a spin or cooking class. Many organizations also offer virtual options, through online workout sessions or video-led teaching. Whatever your hobby, find a way to make it a regularly scheduled part of your week and then defend that time.

Then, communicate with your family about this time and make arrangements. Before the Covid pandemic, my weekly Monday night volleyball league was my haven. I could concentrate on the game, exercise, and enjoy time with friends. The fact that Monday night was volleyball night meant that my wife and I would schedule around it, making it much more likely that I could make almost every session. I got my work done ahead of time or saved tasks for Tuesday. Sometimes we hired a sitter for our son. Once the pandemic hit and I was no longer able to get to the volleyball court, I made regular time for other hobbies, including Wednesday night Zoom happy hour with several local friends and a beer, and solo bike rides around my neighborhood. I'm a much better husband

and father when I get to take an occasional break, and I'm a better professor for my students when I get enough time away.

Obviously, picking up or recommitting to a hobby won't solve all of your work-life balance challenges. But a hobby can be one important part of the puzzle. Work-life balance is a multivariate problem requiring a multi-faceted solution. By scheduling some time for our own needs, we get better at rising to the challenge.

Adapted from "Working Parents, Save Time for Hobbies," on hbr.org, May 7, 2020 (product #H05KX8).

Make Friendships a Part of Your Routine

by Neal J. Roese and Kyle S. H. Dobson

Quick Takes

- Don't use lack of time as an excuse
- Create shared experiences by doing tasks at the same time
- Bundle mundane life activities
- Show friends what's really happening in your life
- Embrace tech options, including video calls and chat apps

Monica gently tucks her 2-year-old son, Hudson, into bed. She has just finished up work as a senior manager at a global bank. As she quietly closes the door to her son's bedroom, her mind flips back to the documents she still needs to review in preparation for an early meeting the next morning. She had hoped to call a friend back first, but she just doesn't have the time (or energy) tonight.

For Monica and many other parents managing challenging careers, a fundamental struggle is balancing work versus family. Whether parenting toddlers or teenagers, working parents can find it difficult to divide their time while still feeling successful and committed in both areas. Friendships barely register in this balancing act. That's a big problem. Basic research in psychology shows that friends are a key contributor to not only the mental well-being of working parents but their career success as well.[1]

Friends matter. We share our innermost secrets with our closest friends, and we can count on them in an emergency. Research shows that close friendships are pivotal to both psychological and physical well-being. Close friendships bring stronger emotional well-being.[2] Friends benefit our basic physiology, as shown by studies that link social connections to cellular-level protection against disease. For instance, we are less likely to catch a cold if we have a solid network of friends.[3] Indeed, having a solid friendship network can reduce mortality as much as 50%.[4] Friends also boost work performance. For one thing, friends (who do not work at your company) give you an "outside view" that can unlock new insights and open your eyes to broader perspectives. For another, friends are a stress reducer. A happy hour after work with friends after a challenging workday, even virtually, may calm the mind as well as the body.

Even if parents recognize the importance of their friends, it's all too easy to let those get-togethers fall to the bottom of the priority list. In fact, the time spent with friends drops steadily over our lifespan; from its peak in the teen years, the fastest decline happens in our 20s and 30s, which is precisely the age range in which children first enter our lives.

So what can we do?

Friendships are nurtured by simple shared experience, like attending the same class, sweating at the same gym, or even sharing the same elevator in your apartment complex. So, it is no surprise that friendships are reinforced through focused sharing—think book clubs and wine-tasting events. But staging these focused get-togethers is tough when you have children, and tougher still when your best friend lives on the other side of the continent—or the planet.

The solution we are exploring in our scholarly research is one we call *bundling*. Bundling is the creation of shared experience by way of combining, or bundling together, two friends' mundane life tasks. Rather than carving out unique time for a book club, pick a task that you do anyway on your own, like shopping for groceries, cooking dinner, or even reading bedtime stories. Then, connect it with a friend who is doing that same thing by using technology. For instance, when it's time to shop for groceries, shop at the same time as your friend and talk to them on your AirPods. When it's time to cook dinner, connect with your friend on FaceTime and share your kitchen tricks on video. When it's time to read a bedtime story to your kids, connect on Zoom and let your friend's kids listen in. The special sauce behind bundling is that you need not be in the same place, just the same time.

Bundling allows us to include friends in our messy lives. Unlike a happy hour, bundling doesn't sacrifice any of our precious free time—and you don't even need to leave the house. Rather, bundling allows us to leverage our current activities as parents to simultaneously strengthen our friendships. Integrating our friends into the necessary parts of our lives makes us more authentic by showing our friends what is really happening behind the scenes (as opposed to the happy front we display in Facebook or Instagram posts). This kind of intimate self-disclosure and vulnerability is a key ingredient for maintaining close relationships. Bundling can be quick, too. It may only take a weekly call while you clean your living room to make you feel close to a friend who lives in another city.

The great news about bundling is that we now live in a time of abundance in tech solutions to help us share our moments. As you consider the power of bundling, the following tech options are just the tip of the iceberg:

- Use Zoom or Skype while cooking. Try cooking or baking the same thing as your friend in real time, all the while watching each other's creations unfold.

- Use Marco Polo to create brief video messages in the moment for viewing by your friend later in the day. Keep it short and keep it real.

- Use noise-canceling earbuds to talk on the phone (yes, the phone) while doing housework, like emptying the dishwasher, doing laundry, or cleaning up.

- Use FaceTime or Duo while grocery shopping. Show off the odd and esoteric items you buy for your kids.

- Simulate the movie theater experience with your family and friend's family. Click play on Hulu or Netflix on the phone at the same time, hang up, and then talk about the movie after it's over. If the movie is a comedy, try adding a voice-only connection to your friend's house so that you can hear the reaction to the funny bits; laughter is infectious.

- Working the same time as friends? Use Slack instead of text messaging to keep each other up to date with your goals, remain focused, and stay connected throughout the workday.

- Make a virtual coffee shop with video and your own home brew.

Parents with careers have an enormous challenge in time management, but that challenge can actually be assisted, not worsened, by taking the time to connect with friends. There are many ways to keep in touch without sacrificing who you are. Encourage your friends to bundle their tasks with you; it may well help both of you without adding any extra effort or stress. Any time you intend to do something alone, ask yourself if there's a way you can include a friend.

Adapted from "Working Parents, Make Friendships a Part of Your Routine," on hbr.org, May 12, 2020 (product #H05LGU).

20

How to Get the Most Out of a Day Off

by Elizabeth Grace Saunders

Quick Takes

- Take "micro-vacations" more regularly
- Use your time off to do nonwork tasks
- Take an hour or two to meet friends
- Reserve time to spend with your spouse or partner
- Work remotely in a serene location for a change of scenery

The idea of "vacation" often conjures up thoughts of trips to faraway lands. While it's true that big trips can be fun and even refreshing, they can also take a lot of time, energy, and money. A lot of people feel exhausted just thinking about planning a vacation—not just navigating personal commitments and school breaks but deciding how to delegate major projects or put work on hold, just so they can have a stress-free holiday. Because of this, some might put off their time away, figuring they'll get to it when their schedule isn't so demanding, only to discover at the end of the year that they haven't used up their paid time off.

In my experience as a time management coach and as a business owner, I've found that vacations don't have to be big to be significant to your health and happiness. In fact, I've been experimenting with the idea of taking "micro-vacations" on a frequent basis, usually every other week. These small bits of time off can increase my sense of happiness and the feeling of having room to breathe.

From my point of view, micro-vacations are times off that require you to use a day or less of vacation time. Because of their shorter duration, they typically require less effort to plan. And micro-vacations usually don't require you to coordinate others taking care of your work while you're gone. Because of these benefits, micro-vacations can happen more frequently throughout the year, which allows you to recharge before you're feeling burned out.

If you're feeling as if you need a break from the day-to-day but can't find the time for an extended vacation, here are four ways to add micro-vacations to your life.

Weekend Trips

Instead of limiting vacations to weeklong adventures, consider a two- to three-day trip to someplace local. I'm blessed to live in Michigan, and one of my favorite weekend trips is to drive to Lake Michigan for some time in a little rented cottage on the shore or to drive up north to a state park. Especially if you live in an urban area, traveling even a few hours can make you feel as if you're in a different world.

To make the trip as refreshing as possible, consider taking time off on Friday so you can wrap up packing, get to your destination, and do a few things before calling it a night. That still leaves you with two days to explore the area. If you get home by dinnertime on Sunday, you can unpack and get the house in order before your workweek starts again.

There may be a few more emails than normal to process on Monday, but other than that, your micro-vacation shouldn't create any big work pileups.

Margin for Personal To-Do Items

Sometimes getting the smallest things done can make you feel fantastic. Consider an afternoon—or even a full day—to take an unrushed approach to all of the nonwork tasks that you really want to do but struggle to find time to do. For example, think of those appointments like getting your hair cut, nails done, oil changed, or doctor visits. You know that you should get these taken care of, but finding the time is difficult with your normal schedule.

Or perhaps you want to take the time to do items that you never seem to get to, like picking out patio furniture, unpacking the remaining boxes in the guest room, or setting up your retirement account. You technically could get these kinds of items done on a weeknight or over the weekend. But if you're consistently finding that you're not and you have vacation time, use it to lift some of the weight from the nagging to-do list.

Shorter Days for Socialization

As individuals get older and particularly after they get married and have children, there tends to be a reduction in how much time they spend with friends. One way to find time for friends without feeling as if you're sacrificing your family time is to take an hour or two off in a day to meet a friend for lunch or to get together with friends before heading home. If you're allowed to split up your vacation time in these small increments, a single vacation day could easily give you four opportunities to connect with friends who you otherwise might not see at all.

If you struggle to have an uninterrupted conversation with your spouse because your kids are always around, a similar strategy can be helpful. Find days when one or both of you can take a little time off to be together. An extra hour or two will barely make a difference at work but could make a massive impact on the quality of your relationship.

Remote Days for Decompression

Many offices offer remote working options for some or all of the week. If working remotely is conducive to your work style and your tasks, take advantage. Working remotely is not technically a micro-vacation, but it can often *feel* like one. If you have a commute of an hour or more each way, not having to commute can add back in two or more hours to your life that can be used for those personal tasks or social times mentioned above.

Also, for individuals who work in places that are loud, lack windows, or where drive-by meetings or chatter are common, working remotely can feel like a welcome respite. Plus, you're likely to get more done. A picturesque location can also give you a new sense of calm as you approach stressful projects. I find that if I'm working in a beautiful setting, like by a lake, it almost feels as good as a vacation. My surroundings have a massive impact on how I feel.

Instead of seeing "vacation" as a large event once or twice a year, consider integrating micro-vacations into your life on a regular basis. By giving yourself permission to take time for yourself, you can increase your sense of ease with your time.

Adapted from content on hbr.org, May 25, 2018 (product #H04CRG).

21

Get in the Right State of Mind for Vacation

by Alexander Caillet, Jeremy Hirshberg, and Stefano Petti

Quick Takes

- Focus on the most critical activities before vacation
- Create a clean work and home environment to return to
- Transition into your vacation slowly
- Disconnect once your vacation starts
- Be present, try new things, and have fun

Have you ever been on vacation and been unable to relax? The whole point of taking time off is to achieve the calm, happy, and energized (CHE) states of mind that make us most productive and effective both while we're away and when we're back in the office and our daily routines. So how can you make sure that happens?

Stage 1: Prepare

Prepping for a vacation can be stressful. From scheduling time that aligns with school schedules and extracurriculars, planning activities, and packing bags to figuring out whether and how to complete, delegate, delay, or drop work, such steps can generate anxiety, frustration, and even anger. But if you succumb to these unproductive states of mind, you exacerbate the problem: You'll be less likely to get everything done and leave yourself more to worry about while on holiday. Even during this period of scrambling, you must work toward CHE by focusing on only the most critical activities, ignoring distractions, and taking regular breaks that allow you to breathe, stretch your body, clear your mind, reflect, and socialize—all proven techniques for inspiring higher states of mind.

Right before you leave, create a work and home environment that will offer you a clear slate upon return: clean out the fridge; tidy up your living space; work ahead on assignments for your job, so deadlines aren't missed; set an out-of-office message on your email; and recruit friends or coworkers to help out while you're away. This type of thoughtful planning will augment your chances of maintaining a higher state of mind upon your return.

Stage 2: Transition

As you start your vacation, you'll want to relax as quickly as possible. After all, you're away from home (or at least away from the daily grind, if you've chosen a "staycation") and finally have time for yourself and your family. But a more effective approach is to transition slowly, allowing your mind and body to get used to the change, particularly if your prep time was very stressful. Research shows that stress can dampen our immune system. It's true that stress hormones like cortisol prop us up for a time. But if we relax too quickly, letting go of that support before our immune system can recuperate, we can expose ourselves to illness. So, maintain a similar level of mental and physical activity for the first few days of your holiday and then ease into full relaxation.

Stage 3: Vacation

Once you're immersed in your holiday, operate in ways that will lead you to CHE:

- **Disconnect.** Stop checking emails, calls, and texts, allowing only emergency information to come through. Let go of anything over which you have no control.

- **Be present.** Truly appreciate each moment. Center yourself with pauses similar to the ones you should take at work but make them longer. Breathe in and out for a total of 10 seconds, check your body and ease any discomfort with stretching or movement, clear your mind, then activate a positive feeling of appreciation and gratitude for where you are at the moment.

- **Focus on health.** Eat nutritious food, drink lots of water, exercise, and sleep. Take care of yourself.

- **Try new experiences.** While away, try new experiences. This can include eating new foods, attending cultural events, engaging in physical activities, and taking part in challenging adventures. Move

Can I Really Unplug?

by Alexandra Samuel

No one wants to be the parent who is staring at their phone during holiday, missing memories in the making, but sometimes the prospect of cutting off all access to technology can cause more stress than if you just logged on to work once in a while. Make a plan for how much (or how little) you can use your devices during your time off by asking yourself these questions:

What's the least amount of work connectivity I can get away with? Understand your office culture and separate your colleagues' expectations from your own anxiety. What is the minimum connectivity that will be accepted at your job?

What do I still want to use technology for while I'm away? Make a list of the specific ways you want to use your phone, tablet, or computer while you're on vacation and limit your tech use to what's on that list. For example, I use the app Roadtrippers to organize my family's itinerary and activities, an Evernote notebook as my personal guidebook, Yelp as a travel journal, and Facebook to stay in touch with friends.

(continued)

Can I Really Unplug?

Which accounts will I disconnect from? It's easier to disconnect from entire networks or accounts than to ignore work-related correspondence once it hits your radar. Once you know what you want to keep doing—and how much you can stop doing—identify which accounts you'll stay away from and plan accordingly, setting up vacation messages or alerts as necessary.

What do I and my fellow travelers expect from one another? Explain your technology game plan to friends and family. Agree on when it is and isn't OK to use your devices—for example, you may agree that it's fine to read the morning news on your tablet over breakfast, but not OK to look at sports scores over dinner. Setting shared expectations about tech use is especially important if you have kids you're trying to keep offline or off-screen.

Asking these questions will help you disconnect without the additional stress, and you'll be able to relax even with your devices in tow.

Adapted from "The Right Way to Unplug When You're on Vacation," on hbr.org, July 15, 2014 (product #H00WMR).

outside your zone of operation and take a few risks to increase your sense of being alive.

- **Really have fun.** Ensure that laughter and smiles are part of your daily routine. Ask yourself: What will make this a special vacation? What is possible for me today? What really matters right now? What can I do to feel joyful, fulfilled, and rejuvenated?

Your state of mind before and during vacation determines the quality of and benefits derived from your time off. Make sure to stay calm, happy, and energized through your prep, your transition and, finally, your well-deserved holiday. With restorative time off, you're more likely to feel refreshed and be productive when you return to work and daily life.

Adapted from content posted on hbr.org, June 29, 2015.

Epilogue

Try It, You Might Like It

22

It's Not Selfish to Take Care of Yourself

by Stewart D. Friedman

Quick Takes

- It's easy to ignore self-care, since you're only accountable to yourself

- Neglecting your own needs can lead to burnout

- Practicing self-care will help you perform better

- Experiment and see how it feels

One of the most compelling findings my colleague Jeff Greenhaus and I reported in our book *Work and Family—Allies or Enemies?* on the lives and careers of over 800 business professionals was this: The more time that working mothers spent taking care of themselves, the better the emotional and physical health of their children.

Does this apparent paradox surprise you? It shouldn't, for it's just another bit of proof that if you don't take care of yourself, then you can't really serve those who depend on you. But when I ask participants in my Total Leadership program to rate how they feel about things in the four main parts of their lives—work, home, community, and self—it's often the last that's rated lowest.

Why is it so difficult for people—mothers *and* fathers—to devote the resources needed to take care of themselves?

It's easiest to ignore the self because the only one to whom you're accountable is you. In the face of intense pressure to meet the performance expectations of the people around you at work, at home, and in the community, you're naturally inclined to give yourself short shrift. Focusing time and attention on yourself is too readily construed as being, well, selfish—so you're likely to feel guilty if you do. Unfortunately, while it might seem noble in the short run to sacrifice the needs you have to cultivate your mind, body, and spirit, over time it's a recipe for burnout. A sustainable life as a leader who contributes meaningfully to the world requires the discipline to take care of you, too.

How, then, to overcome the guilt? The key is to very specifically identify how, by better meeting the expectations you have for enhancing your mind, your body, and your spirit, you are indeed making things better at work, at home, and in the community.

It's not that hard: Just think, for example, about how you're more likely to perform better at work *and* at home *and* in the community—according to the standards of those who evaluate you in these different domains— if you get a full night's rest, exercise regularly, eat well, meditate, do yoga, take a walk, listen to music, or do whatever it is that rejuvenates and restores you. Try it for a month or so, making sure to assess the impact of your experiment on your performance. If you've designed it well, with the interests of your key stakeholders in mind, then you'll probably find that by taking better care of yourself, you're better able to get the results you want in serving others.

After doing experiments like these, I ask participants in my program to rate their satisfaction in all four areas of life again. The biggest jump is in the domain of "self"—by an average increase of 39%! And their satisfaction goes up while their performance improves across all domains, too.

What have you done recently to take better care of yourself and strengthen your ability to perform well in the other parts of your life? In these stressful times, it's more important than ever that we all do so.

Adapted from "Why It's Not Selfish to Take Care of Yourself," on hbr.org, September 18, 2008 (product #H0026M).

NOTES

Chapter 2

1. Kristen M. Shockley, Winny Shen, Michael M. DeNunzio, Maryana L. Arvan, and Eric A. Knudsen, "Disentangling the Relationship between Gender and Work–Family Conflict: An Integration of Theoretical Perspectives Using Meta-analytic Methods," *Journal of Applied Psychology* 102, no. 12 (2017): 1601–1635.

2. Sarah Thébaud and David S. Pedulla, "Masculinity and the Stalled Revolution: How Gender Ideologies and Norms Shape Young Men's Responses to Work–Family Policies," *Gender & Society* 30, no. 4 (2016): 590–617; Scott Behson, "What's a Working Dad to Do?" hbr.org, August 21, 2013, https://hbr.org/2013/08/whats-a-working-dad-to-do; Gayle Kaufman, "Barriers to Equality: Why British Fathers Do Not Use Parental Leave," *Community, Work & Family* 21, no. 3 (2018): 310–325.

3. Stewart D. Friedman and Alyssa Westring, "Empowering Individuals to Integrate Work and Life: Insights for Management Development," *Journal of Management Development* 34, no. 3 (April 2015): 299–315.

Chapter 4

1. Amy Edmondson, "Building a Psychologically Safe Workplace," TEDx, May 4, 2014, https://www.youtube.com/watch?v=LhoLuui9gX8&t=4s.

Chapter 5

1. Andrew J. Oswald, Eugenio Proto, and Daniel Sgroi, "Happiness and Productivity," *Journal of Labor Economics* 33, no. 4 (2015): 789–822.

Chapter 7

1. Pew Research Center, "Breadwinner Moms," *Social & Demographic Trends*, May 29, 2013, https://www.pewsocialtrends.org/2013/05/29/breadwinner-moms/5/; Pew Research Center, "Modern Parenthood," *Social & Demographic Trends*, March 14, 2013, https://www.pewsocialtrends.org/2013/03/14/modern-parenthood-roles-of-moms-and-dads-converge-as-they-balance-work-and-family/; Brad Harrington, Fred Van Deusen, and Jennifer Sabatini Fraone, "The New Dad: A Work (and Life) in Progress," Boston College Center for Work & Family, 2013, https://www.bc.edu/content/dam/files/centers/cwf/research/publications3/researchreports/The%20New%20Dad%202013_A%20Work%20and%20Life%20in%20Progress.

2. Scott Behson, *The Working Dad's Survival Guide: How to Succeed at Work and at Home* (Melbourne, FL: Motivational Press, 2015).

Chapter 8

1. Samuel S. Monfort, Hannah E. Stroup, and Christian E. Waugh, "The Impact of Anticipating Positive Events on Responses to Stress," *Journal of Experimental Social Psychology* 58 (2015): 11–22.

Chapter 9

1. Francis J. Flynn, D. Newark, and V. Bohns, "Once Bitten, Twice Shy: The Effect of a Past Refusal on Future Compliance," *Social Psychology and Personality Science* 5, no. 2 (2014).

2. Lara B. Aknin et al., "Making a Difference Matters: Impact Unlocks the Emotional Benefits of Prosocial Spending," *Journal of Economic Behavior and Organization* 88 (2013): 90–95.

Chapter 10

1. Timothy Ketelaar and Wing Tung Au, "The Effects of Feelings of Guilt on the Behaviour of Uncooperative Individuals in Re-

peated Social Bargaining Games: An Affect-as-Information Interpretation of the Role of Emotion in Social Interaction," *Cognition and Emotion* 17, no. 3 (2003): 429–453.

2. Ronda L. Fee and June P. Tangney, "Procrastination: A Means of Avoiding Guilt or Shame?," *Journal of Social Behavior and Personality* 15, no. 5 (2000): 167–184.

3. S. C. Hayes, "Acceptance and Commitment Therapy and the New Behavior Therapies: Mindfulness, Acceptance, and Relationship," in *Mindfulness and Acceptance: Expanding the Cognitive-Behavioral Tradition*, S. C. Hayes et al., eds. (New York: Guilford Press, 2004), 1–29.

Chapter 11

1. Corinna Reichl, Michael P. Leiter, and Frank M. Spinath, "Work–Nonwork Conflict and Burnout: A Meta-Analysis," *Human Relations* 67, no. 8 (2014): 979–1005.

2. Ute R. Hülsheger et al., "Benefits of Mindfulness at Work: The Role of Mindfulness in Emotion Regulation, Emotional Exhaustion, and Job Satisfaction," *Journal of Applied Psychology* 98, no. 2 (2013): 310–325.

Chapter 13

1. Daphne M. Davis and Jeffrey A. Hayes, "What Are the Benefits of Mindfulness?" *Monitor on Psychology* 43, no. 7 (2012): 64.

2. Pew Research Center, "Raising Kids and Running a Household: How Working Parents Share the Load," *Social and Demographic Trends*, November 4, 2015, https://www.pewsocialtrends.org/2015/11/04/raising-kids-and-running-a-household-how-working-parents-share-the-load/.

3. Harvard Medical School, "In the Journals: Mindfulness Meditation Practice Changes the Brain," *Harvard Women's Health Watch*, April 2011.

Chapter 14

1. Carl J. Caspersen, Kenneth E. Powell, and Gregory M. Christenson, "Physical Activity, Exercise, and Physical Fitness: Definitions and Distinctions for Health-Related Research," *Public Health Reports* 100, no. 2 (1985): 126–131.

Chapter 16

1. William J. Strawbridge, Sarah J. Schema, and Robert E. Roberts, "Impact of Spouses' Sleep Problems on Partners," *Sleep* 27, no. 3 (May 2004): 527–531; Amie M. Gordon and Serena Chen, "The Role of Sleep in Interpersonal Conflict: Do Sleepless Nights Mean Worse Fights?," *Social Psychology and Personality Science* 5, no. 2 (2014): 168–175; Angela M. Hicks and Lisa M. Diamond, "Don't Go to Bed Angry: Attachment, Conflict, and Affective and Physiological Reactivity," *Personal Relationships* 18, no. 2 (2011): 266–284.

2. Mona El-Sheikh et al., "Marital Conflict and Disruption of Children's Sleep," *Child Development* 77, no. 1 (2006): 31–43; Chrystyna D. Kouros and Mona El-Sheikh, "Within-Family Relations in Objective Sleep Duration, Quality, and Schedule," *Child Development* 6, no. 6 (2007): 1983–2000; Annie Bernier et al., "Mothers, Fathers, and Toddlers: Parental Psychosocial Functioning as a Context for Young Children's Sleep," *Developmental Psychology* 49, no. 7 (2013): 1375–1384.

3. Lucy S. King et al., "Mothers' Postpartum Sleep Disturbance Is Associated with the Ability to Sustain Sensitivity toward Infants," *Sleep Medicine* 65 (2010): 74–83; Teresa A. Lillis et al., "Sleep Quality Buffers the Effects of Negative Social Interactions on Maternal Mood in the 3–6 Month Postpartum Period: A Daily Diary Study," *Journal of Behavioral Medicine* 41 (2018): 733–746.

4. Christopher M. Barnes, "Research: Your Abusive Boss Is Probably an Insomniac," *Harvard Business Review*, November 2014; Cristiano Guarana and Christopher M. Barnes, "Research: Sleep

Deprivation Can Make It Harder to Stay Calm at Work," *Harvard Business Review*, August 2017; Christopher M. Barnes, "Research: Sleep-Deprived Leaders Are Less Inspiring," *Harvard Business Review*, June 2016; Christopher M. Barnes and Nathaniel F. Watson, "Why Healthy Sleep Is Good for Business," *Sleep Medicine Reviews* 47 (2019): 112–118.

Chapter 17

1. Robert Half, "9 in 10 Employees Come to Work Sick, Survey Shows," press release, October 24, 2019, http://rh-us.mediaroom .com/2019-10-24-9-In-10-Employees-Come-To-Work-Sick-Survey -Shows.

2. Alexander Kunst, "Number of Sick Days Taken by U.S. Adults in the Past Year as of 2017, by Age," Statista, September 23, 2019, https://www.statista.com/statistics/682924/sick-leave-days-among -adults-us-by-age/.

Chapter 19

1. Sara B. Algoe, "Positive Interpersonal Processes," *Current Directions in Psychological Science* 28, no. 2 (2019): 183–188; Amy E. Colbert, Joyce E. Bono, and Radostina K. Purvanova, "Flourishing via Workplace Relationships: Moving Beyond Instrumental Support," *Academy of Management Journal* 59, no. 4 (2015).

2. Kennon M. Sheldon and Tan H. Hoon, "The Multiple Determination of Well-Being: Independent Effects of Positive Traits, Needs, Goals, Selves, Social Supports, and Cultural Contexts," *Journal of Happiness Studies* 8 (2007): 565–592.

3. Sheldon Cohen et al., "Sociability and Susceptibility to the Common Cold," *Psychological Science* 14, no. 5 (2003): 389–395.

4. Julianne Holt-Lunstad, "Why Social Relationships Are Important for Physical Health: A Systems Approach to Understanding and Modifying Risk and Protection," *Annual Review of Psychology* 69 (2018): 437–458.

ABOUT THE CONTRIBUTORS

DAISY DOWLING, SERIES EDITOR, is the founder and CEO of Workparent, the executive coaching and training firm, and the author of *Workparent: The Complete Guide to Succeeding on the Job, Staying True to Yourself, and Raising Happy Kids* (Harvard Business Review Press, 2021). She is a full-time working parent to two young children. She can be reached at www.workparent.com.

CHRISTOPHER M. BARNES is a professor of organizational behavior at the University of Washington's Foster School of Business. He worked in the Fatigue Countermeasures branch of the Air Force Research Laboratory before pursuing his PhD in Organizational Behavior at Michigan State University and has kept sleep as his primary research interest. He has twin infants and a preschooler and thus understands sleep deprivation from an experiential perspective as well.

SCOTT BEHSON is a professor of management at Fairleigh Dickinson University and the author of *The Working Dad's Survival Guide* and the forthcoming book *The Family-Forward Workplace*. He writes and consults on work-life policies and has been a featured speaker at both the White House and United Nations. His most important roles are as husband and father. He can be seen most often writing in the car during his teen son's sports practices.

ALICE BOYES, PhD, is a former clinical psychologist turned writer and is author of *The Healthy Mind Toolkit* and *The Anxiety Toolkit*. She is mom to a 4-year-old daughter.

ALEXANDER CAILLET is the CEO of Corentus, Inc., an international professional services firm dedicated to team and leadership development. An organizational psychologist, he is on the faculty of Georgetown University's Institute for Transformational Leadership and its Leadership Coaching program. Born in France, Alexander currently lives in the United States and has lived and worked in over 30 countries.

RUSSELL CLAYTON is a faculty member at the Muma College of Business at the University of South Florida and a cofounder of Work-Life Insights, a training and continuing education firm. He is also a husband and father of two wonderful daughters. When he is not teaching or leading a workshop, you can often find him with his family at the beach or Disney World. Connect with him at www.worklifeinsights.com.

JACKIE COLEMAN is a former marriage counselor and most recently worked on education programs for the state of Georgia. She and her husband John have three wonderful kids under 7, who keep them up to date on all things Pokémon, Fancy Nancy, and Old MacDonald's farm.

JOHN COLEMAN is a coauthor of the book *Passion and Purpose: Stories from the Best and Brightest Young Business Leaders* (Harvard Business Review Press, 2012). He is the father of three wonderful children, with his wife Jackie. Follow him on Twitter @johnwcoleman.

NICK CROCKER is a general partner at Blackbird Ventures and runs the firm's Melbourne office. He is a cofounder and former CEO of Sessions, a personal coaching program that uses technology to help people live better, healthier lives. His writing has been published in *Wired, Fast Company,* and *Harvard Business Review.* Follow him on Twitter @nickcrocker.

KYLE S. H. DOBSON is a postdoctoral research fellow at the University of Texas at Austin's Population Research Center. Although he doesn't have children of his own yet, he treasures the time he gets to talk about his mutual love of superheroes and Pokémon with his best friend's children.

STEWART D. FRIEDMAN, an organizational psychologist at the Wharton School, is author of three Harvard Business Review Press books—*Total Leadership*, *Leading the Life You Want*, and *Parents Who Lead*. He founded the Wharton Leadership Program, the Wharton Work/Life Integration Project, and Total Leadership, a management consulting and training company. His three grown children work in education. He hopes his two grandchildren will help us all heal our broken world.

MICHELLE GALE is a chief of staff at Autodesk, where she founded Autodesk Pause, a mindfulness community. In her spare time, she practices parenting two teenage boys with awareness, curiosity, and plenty of humor.

FRANCESCA GINO is a behavioral scientist and the Tandon Family Professor of Business Administration at Harvard Business School. She is the author of the books *Rebel Talent* and *Sidetracked: Why Our Decisions Get Derailed, and How We Can Stick to the Plan*. Follow her on Twitter @francescagino.

AMIE M. GORDON is an assistant professor of psychology at the University of Michigan, Ann Arbor, where she directs the Well-being, Health, and Interpersonal Relationships Lab (WHIRL). She received her PhD in social-personality psychology from the University of California, Berkeley. As a working mother who functions best on nine hours of sleep, much of her research on sleep and its effects on relationships has been inspired by her own nights of sleep deprivation.

HEIDI GRANT is a social psychologist who researches, writes, and speaks about the science of motivation. She is the director of research & development, EY Americas Learning, and serves as associate director of Columbia's Motivation Science Center. She received her doctorate in social psychology from Columbia University. Her most recent book is *Reinforcements: How to Get People to Help You* (Harvard Review Press, 2018). She is also the author of *Nine Things Successful People Do Differently* (Harvard Business Review Press, 2012) and *No One Understands You and What to Do About It* (Harvard Business Review Press, 2015).

JOSEPH GRENNY is a four-time *New York Times* best-selling author, keynote speaker, and leading social scientist for business performance. His work has been translated into 28 languages, is available in 36 countries, and has generated results for 300 of the *Fortune* 500. He is the cofounder of VitalSmarts, an innovator in corporate training and leadership development.

JEREMY HIRSHBERG, PhD, is a leadership and organizational development consultant. He lives in Southern California with his wife, Shelley, and two boys, Miles and Eli.

ART MARKMAN, PhD, is the Annabel Irion Worsham Centennial Professor of Psychology, Marketing, and Human Dimensions of Organizations at the University of Texas at Austin and executive director of the IC² Institute. He has written over 150 scholarly papers on topics including reasoning, decision making, and motivation. His most recent book is *Bring Your Brain to Work* (Harvard Business Review Press, 2019).

BRITTNEY MAXFIELD is the senior director of marketing communications at VitalSmarts. She is also a busy mom to three brilliant children, ages 8, 6, and 2. Her evenings are jam-packed with homework, soccer games, piano practice, and finding the closest drive-through everyone can agree on. And, despite the chaos, she wouldn't have it any other way.

KATE NORTHRUP is the bestselling author of *Do Less* and *Money: A Love Story.* Her digital company helps ambitious women light up the world without burning themselves out. Learn more at katenorthrup.com.

STEFANO PETTI is a partner at Asterys, an international organizational development firm, and the coauthor of *AEquacy: The New Human-Centered Organization Design to Thrive in a Complex World.* Born in Italy, married to a proud Swede, and parent to two young kids, he is a passionate lifelong learner and explorer.

NEAL J. ROESE is the SC Johnson Chair in Global Marketing at the Kellogg School of Management at Northwestern University and the author of *If Only: How to Turn Regret into Opportunity.* He is the father of two college-age daughters.

ALEXANDRA SAMUEL is a speaker, researcher, and writer who works with the world's leading companies to understand their online customers and craft data-driven reports like "Sharing Is the New Buying." Alex is the author of *Work Smarter with Social Media* (Harvard Business Review Press, 2015); her new class, Work Productivity: Work Smarter with Your Inbox, is now available on Skillshare. Follow Alex on Twitter @awsamuel.

ELIZABETH GRACE SAUNDERS is a time management coach and the founder of Real Life E Time Coaching & Speaking. She is author of *How to Invest Your Time Like Money* and *Divine Time Management.* Find out more at www.RealLifeE.com.

AMY JEN SU is a cofounder and managing partner of Paravis Partners, a premier executive coaching and leadership development firm. For the past two decades, she has coached CEOs, executives, and rising stars in organizations. She is the author of the Harvard Business Review Press book *The Leader You Want to Be* and coauthor of *Own the Room* with Muriel Maignan Wilkins. Amy is also a full-time working parent with a teenage son who is currently in high school.

TIM SULLIVAN is a publisher and the former editorial director of Harvard Business Review Press. He is the coauthor of *The Org* and *The Inner Lives of Markets*. He has also co-parented five children all the way to adulthood and knows he's not done yet. You can follow him on Twitter @Tim_Org.

MONIQUE VALCOUR is an executive coach, keynote speaker, and management professor. She helps clients create and sustain fulfilling and high-performance jobs, careers, workplaces, and lives. Her greatest joy in life is talking and laughing with her husband and two adult daughters. Follow her on Twitter @moniquevalcour.

ALYSSA F. WESTRING is the Vincent de Paul Associate Professor of Management and Entrepreneurship at DePaul University's Driehaus College of Business. She is the coauthor of *Parents Who Lead* (Harvard Business Review Press, 2020). She is an award-winning educator and is director of research at Total Leadership. She has two school-age children and lives in Chicago.

INDEX

acceptance, 78–79, 97–98
accomplishments,
    acknowledging, 31, 78
accountability, 8, 30, 170–171
alone time, 8, 26

balance, 51
    conversations for, 45–51
    Covid pandemic and, 83
    exercise and, 110–111
    self-care and, xiii–xviii
    talking about at work,
        56–58
Bandura, Albert, 112
Barnes, Christopher M.,
    121–129
bedtime routines, 124–125
Behson, Scott, 53–58, 139–145
Boyes, Alice, xvii–xviii, 91–100
breaks, xiv, 6
    for exercise, 113
    from exercise, 117
    micro-, 7–8
    micro-vacations and, 153–
        158
    weaving into your workday,
        32
Bridge of Spies (movie), 76
bundling, 150–152
burnout, 4, 81–89

Caillet, Alexander, 159–165
Caspersen, Carl J., 111
catastrophizing, 93–94
changes, starting with
    small, 7–8
children
    affirming, 5–6
    communicating openly with,
        23, 49–51, 136
    health of, 136, 170
    mealtimes and, 129
    quality time with, 5–6, 39
    scheduling time with, 25–26
    sick days and, 136
    sleep deprivation and, 123
    sleep routines for, 124–125
    spending time with, through
        hobbies, 142–145
chores, 39
    with friends, 150–152
Clayton, Russell, 109–114
Coleman, Jackie, 59–66
Coleman, John, 61
Collins, Caitlyn, 98–99
commitment, 8, 143–144
communication
    about schedules, 23–26
    about self-care needs, 59–66
    about sick days, 134, 136
    about work-life balance at
        work, 56–58

communication (*continued*)
  asking for help, 67–72
  with children, 23, 49–51, 136
  clarity in, 69–70
  crucial conversations in,
    45–51
  of gratitude, 72
  guilt/shame and, 61
  "I feel" statements for, 64
  listening in, 64–65
  soft startups in, 64
  with spouses/partners, 49,
    59–66, 135
  timing for, 63, 127
  for working dads, about
    work, 53–58
  with your boss and
    colleagues, 47–48, 135
  with your inner perfectionist,
    95–96
compassion, 77, 94, 96
couple time, 9–10. *See also*
  spouse/partners
Covid pandemic, xvii–xviii, 60
  emotional exhaustion in, 83
  hobbies during, 144–145
  remote work during, 83
  stress management and, 85, 88
  taking sick days and, 132–133
Crocker, Nick, xvii, 115–119

dads
  communicating about work
    by, 53–58
  self-care for, 11–17

time spent with children
  and, 55
work-family conflict
  experienced by, 12
Dobson, Kyle S. H., 147–152
Dowling, Daisy, xiii–xviii
dual-income families, 55

Edmondson, Amy, 30
Emmons, Robert, 86–87
emotional well-being, xvii
  conserving energy and, 84,
    85, 88
  doing less and, 36–41
  friendships and, 148–149
  gratitude and, 72, 86–87
  guilt and, 75–79
  hobbies and, 141
  mindfulness and, 101–105
  perfectionism and, 91–100
  permission to recharge and,
    3–10
  productivity and, 40–41
  recharging and, 14–15, 81–89
  reducing emotional drain
    and, 83–85
  self-care and, 60, 62, 170
  talking with children about,
    50–51
empathy, 65
exercise, xvii
  breaks from, 117
  commitment to, 8
  emotional well-being and,
    88–89

enjoying, 118
expectations about, 116–117
finding time for, 112–113,
    115–119
goals in, 118
importance of, 109–114
scheduling, 25
starting small with, 7
walking meetings and,
    32
yoga, 96

family leave, 56
fatigue, xiv, 128–129. *See also*
    sleep
emotional, 81–89
fathers. *See* dads
"The Flexibility Stigma," 55–56
flexible work arrangements,
    47–48
exercise and, 113
for men, 56, 57
remote working, 157–158
sleep and, 129
focus, 36
four-way wins, 13–14
Friedman, Stewart D., 11–17,
    169–172
friendships, 6, 147–152
bundling, 150–152
emotional well-being and,
    88–89
hobbies and, 142–145
micro-vacations with,
    156–157

supporting spouse/partner's,
    9–10
weaving into your workday,
    31
at work, 97–98
fun, 165

Gale, Michelle, 101–105
Gandhi, Mahatma, 57
gender norms, 53–55, 99–100
Gino, Francesca, 86–87
goals
acknowledging progress
    toward, 31
for exercise, 118
for self-care, 61, 63
setting daily, 30
setting with spouses/
    partners, 49
for values-driven schedules,
    21, 22
Gordon, Amie M., 121–129
Gottman, John, 64
Grant, Heidi, 67–72
gratitude, 72, 86–87
Greenhaus, Jeff, 170
Grenny, Joseph, 45–51
guilt, 46, 61, 75–79, 170–171
perfectionism and, 94
shame vs., 76–77
sick days and, 132–133

habits
personal fulfillment and, 62

habits (*continued*)
  sleep, 124–127
  unproductive, 34
health. *See* emotional well-
    being; physical health
help, asking for, 67–72
Hirshberg, Jeremy, 159–165
hobbies, 6, 139–145
household tasks. *See* chores
humor, 95–96

"I feel" statements, 64
income, 12, 51, 55, 56
intentionality, 20

Journal of Social Issues, 55–
  56
judgment, 29
  asking for help and, 70–71
  holding back on, 128
  of self, 30, 93–94
  of women's *vs.* men's
    mistakes, 99–100

Kabat-Zinn, Jon, 102

life satisfaction, 13–14, 16, 60,
    62, 171–172
  gratitude and, 86–87
listening, 64–65

Markman, Art, 75–79
Maxfield, Brittney, 45–51
McCollough, Michael,
    86–87
meals and mealtimes, 129
mental health days, 134
micro-breaks, 7–8. *See also*
    breaks
mindfulness, 78–79, 89, 101–
    105
  benefits of, 102, 104–105
  perfectionism and, 96
mistakes
  moving on from, exercise
    and, 117
  perfectionism and, 91–100
motherhood penalty, 51
Mother's Day, 12
motivation
  guilt and, 76–77, 79
  perfectionism and, 94

needs, xvii. *See also* values
  asking for help and, 67–72
  defining, 69
  defining your self-care,
    6–7
  prioritizing your own, 4
Northrup, Kate, 35–41

Oettingen, Gabriele, 78
overthinking, xv. *See also*
    rumination

parental leave, 12, 57
parenthood and parenting
  big wins in, 39–40
  positive effects of on work, 97
  priority definition for, 20
  quality *vs.* quantity of time
    in, 5–6, 39
  sleep and, 121–129
  transformative nature of, 4
Parents Night Out, 8
paternity leave, 12, 56, 57
perfectionism, xvii–xviii,
  91–100
performance, 30
  exercise and, 113
  friendships and, 149
  self-care and, 171–172
performance evaluations, 12
perspective
  "50-year," 24–25
  focusing on
    accomplishments in, 31, 78
  friendships and, 149
  gratitude and, 86–87
  on priorities, 24–25
  scarcity mindset and, 34
  on stress, 85, 88
Petti, Stefano, 159–165
Pew Research Center, 102
physical health, xvii
  exercise and, 109–114
  gratitude and, 86–87
  recharging and, 16
  self-care and, 170
  sick days and, 131–136

  sleep and, 121–129
  vacations and, 161–162
presence, 5, 102, 162
priorities
  aligning, 110–111
  defining importance of,
    24–25
  determining, 21–23, 30
  doing less and, 35–41
  friendships as, 147–152
  hobbies and, 139–145
  for self-care, 61, 63
  setting daily, 30
  sick days and, 134
  sleep, 123, 124
  time management based on,
    19–26
  worksheet for, 22
problem solving, 142
productivity, xiv, 60, 62
  doing less and, 36–41
  exercise and, 111
  happiness and, 40–41
  sleep and, 124
psychological safety, 30

recharging, 3–10, 32, 81–89
  spillover effect from, 14–15
relaxation, 88–89
resilience, xvii, 86–87
remote work
  Covid pandemic and, 83
  to decompress, 157–158
resources, 30

rituals
  emotional well-being and,
    89
  scheduling, 23
  sleep, 124–125
Rock, David, 36
Roese, Neal J., 147–152
rumination, 94–95

Samuel, Alexandra, 163–164
Saunders, Elizabeth Grace,
    xvii, 3–10, 19–26
scarcity mindset, 34
scheduling, xvii
  hobbies, 143–144
  mindfulness, 103–104
screen time, 125–126
self-acceptance, 97–98
self-care, xiii–xviii
  asking for help and, 67–72
  benefits of, 60, 62
  communicating about your
    needs in, 59–66
  defining, 28
  defining your needs for, 6–7
  importance of, xvi, 28,
    169–172
  noticing lapses in, 33–34
  personal differences in, 29
  sick days and, 131–136
  spillover effects of, 14–15
  starting small with, 7–8
  weaving into your workday,
    27–34
self-compassion, 77, 94, 96

self-criticism, 30, 93–94
self-efficacy, 111–113, 114
selfishness, 170–171
self-knowledge, 47
self-management, 33
self-neglect, 33
self-preservation, 34
self-sabotage, 29, 34
shame, 61, 76, 94
"should," 29
sick days, 131–136
sleep, 6, 32, 121–129
  catching up on, 125
  conflicting schedules for, 128
  habits for, 124–127
  relationship-based strategies
    around, 127–129
soft startups, in conversation,
  64
spirituality, 6
spouses/partners
  communicating self-care
    needs to, 59–66
  communicating with, 49
  give-and-take with, 65
  recharging and, 9–10
  relationship checkups with,
    65–66
  sleep health and, 122–123
  talking with, for values-
    driven schedules, 23
stress and stress management,
  xvii
  exercise and, 111, 114
  lapses in self-care and,
    33–34

mindfulness and, 102
reappraising, 85, 88
recharging and, 16
"third space" and, 62
Su, Amy Jen, 27–34
Sullivan, Tim, 131–136
support, 31
  asking for help and, 67–72

technology
  disconnecting from on
    vacations, 162, 163–164
  friendships and, 151–152
  sick days and, 135
thank yous, 72
"third space," 60, 62
time management, xvii
  doing less and, 35–41
  experimenting with, 13–
    17
  friendships and, 147–152
  giving yourself permission
    to recharge and, 3–10
  for hobbies, 143–145
  small changes for, 7–8
  values-based scheduling for,
    19–26
  weaving self-care your
    workday and, 27–34
  for working dads, 11–17
time off, xvii
  disconnecting during, 162,
    163–164
  frame of mind for, 159–165
  friendships and, 147–152

harassment of fathers at work
  about, 12
hobbies and, 139–145
making the most of, 153–158
micro-vacations, 153–158
preparing for, 160–161
sick days, 131–136
technology use during,
  163–164
transitioning into, 161–162
weekend trips, 155
to-do lists, xiii, 156
Total Leadership, 13–17
Twitter, 102–103

uncertainty, xiii–xiv
  asking for help and, 69–70

vacations. See time off
Valcour, Monique, xvii–xviii,
  81–89
values, xvii
  doing less and, 35–41
  scheduling based on, 19–26
  stress management and,
    85, 88
values-based scheduling,
  19–26

walking meetings, 32
Westring, Alyssa F., 11–17
work. See also time off
  doing less and, 35–41

work (*continued*)
exercise at, 118–119
fitting exercise into,
113–114
focus at, 36
gender norms in, 53–55,
99–100
negotiating schedules/
workloads at, 47–48
psychological detachment
from, 88–89

sleep deprivation and, 123
weaving self-care into, 27–34
*Work and Family—Allies or
Enemies?* (Greenhaus and
Friedman), 170
work satisfaction, 13–14
workspaces, 32

yoga, 96
Your Brain at Work (Rock), 36

Find fulfillment at home and at work with the HBR Working Parents Series

Advice for Working Dads

Advice for Working Moms

Communicate Better with Everyone

Getting It All Done

Managing Your Career

Taking Care of Yourself

Engage with HBR content the way you want, on any device.

With HBR's new subscription plans, you can access world-renowned **case studies** from Harvard Business School and receive **four free eBooks**. Download and customize prebuilt **slide decks and graphics** from our **Visual Library**. With HBR's archive, top 50 best-selling articles, and five new articles every day, HBR is more than just a magazine.

Subscribe Today
hbr.org/success